Napoleon's Army in Russia

THE ILLUSTRATED MEMOIRS OF ALBRECHT ADAM, 1812

Translated by Jonathan North

Pen & Sword

MILITARY

First published in Great Britain in 2005 by Pen & Sword Military
an imprint of Pen & Sword Books Ltd
47 Church Street
Barnsley
South Yorkshire
S70 2AS

ISBN 1-84415-161-1

Printed and bound in Singapore by Kyodo Printing Co. (Singapore) Pte Ltd

Pen & Sword Books Ltd incorporates the Imprints of Pen & Sword Aviation, Pen & Sword Maritime, Pen & Sword Military,
Wharncliffe Local History, Pen and Sword Select, Pen and Sword Military Classics and Leo Cooper.

For a complete list of Pen & Sword titles please contact

PEN & SWORD BOOKS LIMITED
47 Church Street, Barnsley, South Yorkshire, S70 2AS, England
E-mail: enquiries@pen-and-sword.co.uk
Website: www.pen-and-sword.co.uk

Contents

Preface 5

Introduction 7

The Plates 24

Epilogue 168

Select Bibliography 176

Preface

Albrecht Adam was born in Nördlingen, a small free state in southern Germany, on 16 April 1786 to Jeremias Adam and Margaretha Adam. His talent for painting quickly became apparent and as early as 1800 he was painting French troops as they marched and shuffled victoriously through southern Germany. Tutored by Christoph Zwinger in Nuremberg, the young artist made steady progress. In July 1807 he moved to Munich and, two years later, took part in the successful war against Austria. During the course of the campaign he met Prince Eugene de Beauharnais, Napoleon's stepson and Viceroy of Italy. Eugene, who had a Bavarian connection as he had married Princess Auguste of Bavaria in 1806, asked Adam to join his household in October 1809. Later that month, the young artist set out for Italy with a modest salary of 2,400 francs.

In 1812 Adam accompanied Eugene's staff on the expedition to Russia. He attached himself to the Viceroy's Topographical Bureau, a small unit of engineers, cartographers and draughtsmen which had been established in 1801. Adam travelled with the IV Corps and accompanied the army on its long, arduous march on Moscow. Labaume, author of a chilling account of the expedition, was one of his associates.

Not long after reaching Moscow Adam decided to return to Germany, depressed, apparently, with what he had witnessed. As he was not obliged to stay, not being part of the military establishment, he obtained permission to quit the French army on 29 September 1812 and, after a harrowing journey, reached Munich on 23 December, just as the remains of Napoleon's massive army was trickling back over the border into Poland.

In 1815, after peace was restored across an exhausted Europe, Adam returned to Munich and found ample work in the city. With King Maximilian as patron Adam was in a privileged position and was able to execute a number of works for the king as well as for the Wrede, Leuchtenberg, Thurn und Taxis, Metternich and Furstenburg families. He was known in particular for his battle scenes but his great passion was for equestrian studies.

In 1827 he began work on the suite of images gathered together under the title of *Voyage pittoresque et militaire*. These plates, reproduced here, were based on sketches he had taken throughout the campaign and are of tremendous historical significance. The work was issued by Hermann and Bath in Munich in 1828 and included in the list of subscribers to the volume were Captain von Faber du Faur and Peter Hess, both celebrated recorders of Napoleon's ill-fated expedition of 1812. Adam says that, originally, the images presented here began life as studies, drawn from his sketches, for large-scale battle scenes. Following the death of Prince Eugene, however, he obtained permission from Eugene's widow to have them published as coloured lithographs. The lithographs are not the only works to stem from Adam's participation in the campaign as he made a number of oil on paper studies before issuing the suite presented here. A number of these images now reside in the Hermitage Museum in St Petersburg.

Because of Adam's Bavarian origins (Nördlingen was absorbed by Bavaria in 1802), and Eugene's Bavarian connection, a number of the lithographs include Bavarian subjects. There are Bavarian troops illustrated in plates 1, 22, 48 and 59, for example. But the majority of the plates illustrate Eugene's Italian troops as they march along Russia's endless highways. Inevitably, the images presented here stop in September 1812, before the legendary retreat. Studying the text and pictures, however, might easily lead to the conclusion that the advance into Russia was just as costly and arduous.

The text is taken from the accompanying text used in the *Voyage pittoresque*. It, in turn, comes from the artist's journal with some borrowings from Labaume and Ségur. The Epilogue, however, is taken from Adam's published memoirs.

Adam died in Munich on 28 August 1862 leaving two sons one of whom, Benno, had been born on 15 July 1812.

Particular thanks must go to Digby Smith, Yves Martin, Dr Thomas Hemmann and Massimo Fiorentino for their considerable assistance. I am also grateful to Rupert Harding, for his enthusiasm, and Peter Harrington in Rhode Island.

But I owe especial thanks to my wife, Evgenia, and to my son, Alexander, for their patience.

Jonathan North
2005

Introduction

In the early summer of 1812 masses of troops were gathering. In Poland and eastern Prussia Napoleon's army, one of the largest ever assembled, began to take up positions along the borders of the Russian empire. Across that border, in Russian-dominated Lithuania, the Czar's troops were also mobilising. The scene was set for an epic confrontation as two empires were set on a collision course and two emperors, once allies, now rivals, gambled on war to maintain or augment their power.

As recently as 1807 the French emperor and the Czar of all the Russias had met and formed an alliance, effectively carving up Europe between them. France rejoiced in power over Germany and Poland whilst Russia set about relieving Sweden of Finland and a series of wars with the Ottoman Porte. Gradually, but perceptively, the two emperors began to bicker. Napoleon's plans for Russia did not conform with Russia's plans, whilst Napoleon's power in Europe seemed interfering, menacing and on the increase.

By 1811, an ugly year of rumour, both sides were preparing for a confrontation. Efforts were made to resolve differences but Napoleon, a man of war, trusted to his armies to bring Russia to heel once sweet words were no longer working. As 1811 ended troops were marching east to deliver a fatal blow to Russian military might, thereby forcing Alexander to recognise his role in Napoleonic Europe.

Napoleon invested a massive amount of preparation into this imperial adventure. Supplies, waggons and armaments were despatched eastwards in 1811 and early 1812. Plans were made for the use of rivers to ferry supplies forwards and towns in eastern Prussia and Poland were designated as stockpiles and magazines. Napoleon had also lavished attention on attempting to gauge what lay in store for his men once they crossed the border. Agents were sent into Lithuania and the Ukraine. On 16 November 1811 the Foreign Ministry had written to Bignon, Resident in Warsaw, stating that the emperor wanted 'statistical details of Podolie, Volhynia and the Ukraine; descriptions of the roads; nature of the terrain; the inhabitants; the roads from Lemberg to Kiev and Doubno to Kiev; and the Dnepr river'. Less attention was paid to the question of food and little effort was placed into checking that orders were actually carried out.

Such concerns did not trouble French military planners unduly. They were informed that the campaign should be over quickly. The Russians would be knocked out by one of the greatest armies ever assembled.

The French emperor had troops from nearly every nation in Europe at his disposal as he began to concentrate forces in Germany and Poland in early 1812. By June some 450,000 were available and could call upon reserves and supports on either flank, elements which boosted this total to 600,000 men and 250,000 horses. The majority of the troops were French, or at least serving in French uniform, but a good number were furnished by vassals and allies. There were Italians, Neapolitans, Poles, Bavarians, Badeners, Westphalians, Saxons, Württembergers, troops from smaller German states, troops from the Balkans, Spaniards, Portuguese and Swiss. Even the reluctant Prussians cooperated and the Austrians, so many times an enemy of France, also deployed a force to operate in the Ukraine.

Much of the Grande Armée was young and reluctant – particularly those in the recently expanded armies of the German states and, of course, the Prussians and Austrians. This posed problems in the early stages of the campaign and, for example, on 10 July the 10th Chasseurs were pulled back because 'due to its lack of ability it is not suited to duty in the frontline'. Even so, Napoleon's army was one of the most imposing military hosts ever to take the field and considerable effort had gone into uniforming, equipping and training the troops. War was looked upon eagerly by many. On 12 July Berthier wrote to Napoleon that '35 pupils of the military school had just finished their artillery examination and they fervently request that they might be allowed to serve in the army under you'. Such attitudes were commonplace in an imperial army accustomed to victory.

In terms of turnout and morale the Imperial Guard and I Corps were particularly magnificent, although other formations could also boast fine troops. Count Bourgoing of the Young Guard describes some of Marshal Ney's corps:

> I studied with awe and respect the French line regiments in III Corps. These regiments were formed by men who had come from the Boulogne camps, where they had trained under the eyes of their marshal. There were no youthful faces here, unlike in our Tirailleurs, for these men bore the martial aspect of veterans.

Such a massive force, however, meant that many elements fell far short of the standards set by Napoleon's best. Many of the soldiers in Napoleon's army were reluctant conscripts, and many became even more reluctant as time wore on. Even before the campaign opened desertion was a problem. In March 1812 the 127th Line lost 97 deserters whilst marching from Magdeburg to Stettin. Some contingents were to suffer heavily from desertion and the Bavarians were described as having 'a mania for desertion'. The French army contained an entire division of reformed deserters (32nd Division, XI Corps) and many line regiments had had to absorb such transgressors in the build-up to war, as Marshal Berthier noted to Napoleon in February 1812:

> Sire, the Minister of War has acquainted me with your order, dated 6 February, that 721 deserters, condemned to hard labour, be pardoned and sent on to Wesel. Here they shall be armed and equipped and sent to join the corps currently in Germany. I have the honour of suggesting that these 721 men be assigned to the 4th, 18th and 72nd Line and the 11th Light, which form part of the II Corps of the Observation of the Elbe. These four regiments are the only French regiments in this corps not to have yet received such deserters.

Measures to prevent conscripts making off as the regiments marched to the front were taken but these weren't always successful. A carabineer of the 29th Light was shot in February 1812 to deter further desertions but, that same day, a further 26 men quit the ranks.

The gathering of such a huge force compounded some of the inevitable consequences of bringing vast numbers of soldiers into the deprived regions of Poland – which had suffered a bad harvest in 1811 – and eastern Prussia. This meant that, due largely to its size, the Grande Armée was in difficulty even before the campaign opened. Despite some meticulous planning, impoverished Poland was swamped by an army too vast to feed. Supplies were unevenly distributed, if distributed at all, soldiers lived off a land unable to sustain them, bickering broke out between various units and various nationalities, commanders fretted, deserters made off and Polish peasants clamoured against the 'invading' army. Both Prussia and Poland would suffer horribly from the passage of troops and, even though they were allies, were being stripped of foodstuffs by forced requisitions. On 19 June, for example, Marshal Ney complained to the Crown Prince of Württemberg that the German contingents were ransacking eastern Prussia for supplies:

> The Emperor has received numerous complaints about the conduct of the Württemberg and Saxon troops. He is particularly dissatisfied with the light cavalry brigade which, according to His Majesty, has brought disaster to the Interbourg region.

Emile Venturini, a Lieutenant in the 11th Light, was ordered to requisition cattle on 8 June. He rounded up 3,000 and noted in his memoirs that he had thereby 'reduced between 200 and 300 families to misery'. Even so such measures had proved relatively ineffective and many troops began the campaign on an empty stomach.

In the brilliant sunlight of June 1812 the invasion began. Pouring across the bridges over the Niemen the French host began their attempt to subdue Russia.

The invasion was a shock to the Russians and their intelligence reports had underestimated the forces being brought against them. Alexander I of Russia learnt of the invasion on 24 June whilst at Vilna. He and his generals had concentrated all available troops on the border with Poland, Barclay de Tolly commanding the First Army of 120,000 troops and Bagration leading the Second Army of some 40,000 men. The command structure was not unified, which led to confusion, as did interference by Alexander himself, and, in the first few days of the campaign the Russians beat a poorly co-ordinated retreat. With no clear goal, Barclay fell back towards Drissa, whilst Bagration did his best to elude the French, cover Minsk and prepare to join up with Barclay. Russian headquarters improvised resistance. There was hope that armies in Finland and Walachia, present-day Romania, could be called upon, and militias and volunteers raised; even so, for the time being, Russian generals had to confront overwhelming numbers.

Kovno was occupied by the French and there followed an immediate push for Vilna with the Reserve Cavalry, I Corps and the Imperial Guard. A symbolic victory was gained when the French entered Vilna on 28 June but Napoleon was immediately disappointed to find the Lithuanian capital could only furnish 6,000 rations rather than the 100,000 he had hoped for. The French pushed forwards, seeking to locate and destroy Russian concentrations. Fortunately for the Russians, on 29 June, massive rain storms swept Lithuania and turned the roads into morasses of slippery mud. Ney noted the consequences of the storms in a letter to Berthier on 30 June: 'The rain, which hasn't stopped falling in torrents for the last 12 hours, means that it is impossible for the Army Corps to march along anything other than main roads.' Despite this, Napoleon single-mindedly pushed his troops, and those on his flanks, to get forward, trap and defeat the Russians and finish the campaign in a decisive battle.

As the French advanced, exhausted by forced marches and muddy conditions, and with their draught horses dying in thousands, they found themselves in territory devoid of supplies. The province had supported 150,000 Russians for the last three months and any supplies not being used up then were now burnt by the retreating Russians or rapidly pillaged or destroyed by bands of stragglers or deserters. Marauding had been a problem right from the start of the campaign as men combed Lithuania for food, sparing nothing, pitying nobody. Captain Skeplicki of the

Polish Guard Lancers noted the effect of such disorganisation in a report to General Krasinski:

> It is my duty to inform you, general, that the terrible behaviour of the stragglers is making a bad impression on the inhabitants. I have seen with my own eyes the village of Dousniatoui pillaged by our cuirassiers. They wander around in groups of four, five or six and fear of them has driven the people into the forests.

The army's own supplies were far to the rear, loaded onto slow-moving wagons. Socrate Blanc wrote to his father on 3 July that he saw such massive convoys on the move near Vilkovisky and that, there being no more horses, waggons were being pulled by oxen. The speed of the advance left such convoys in the rear as did the chaos on many of the roads. The Crown Prince of Württemberg wrote to his father the King on 25 June that:

> The tribulations of the previous few days have been excessive and something like half of the strength of the French divisions have been left behind; we have only come through with considerable trouble and thanks to the efforts of our officers and generals, by my presence among the troops and the distribution of brandy. The countless convoys of undisciplined French wagons block the roads continually and serve as serious impediments. I myself have had to act as a kind of baggage master on a number of occasions.

The exhausting march and the lack of supplies to keep the troops going meant that even the normally well-off Imperial Guard was suffering. General Roguet noted, on 30 June, that his troops had 'not had a bread ration for the last three days'. The rigours of such a campaign, combined with the arduous forced marches, proved too much for many of the thousands of young troops in Napoleon's army; Heinrich von Brandt, whose regiment was marching behind the Young Guard, noted that the newly-raised regiments 'were trailing stragglers, who could be seen stretched out along the sides of the road, mixed up with the dead horses'. An observation confirmed by the commander of the Young Guard Division, General Delaborde, in a letter to Berthier on the same day:

> It is with regret that I inform you that three Tirailleurs have died during today's march. The Voltigeur brigade had six dead and one presumed dead. I constantly receive such distressing reports. If you could possibly obtain leave for the division to be quartered in a town for twenty-four hours, our young soldiers would have the chance to recover somewhat. A considerable number are suffering.

Napoleon, now directing operations from the Bishop's Palace in Vilna, continued to pressure the Russians as they withdrew methodically and in good order. Murat was amazed: 'You have no idea of how the Russians are retreating, they leave nothing, absolutely nothing, behind.' Davout, supported by Napoleon's inexperienced brother, Jerome, harried Bagration, and, marching 400 kilometres in just two weeks, pushed the Russian general's troops through Minsk, seizing a considerable Russian depot to the relief of his own troops. But still the Russians were slipping away, and it seemed increasingly difficult for the French to ascertain exactly where the Russians were and what they intended to do. This was partly due to failure on the part of the French light cavalry which, despite numbering 30,000 men and being constantly in the saddle, found intelligence-gathering utterly trying. Light cavalry divisions were given detachments of Polish cavalry, who could interrogate prisoners and relay information from inhabitants, in order to make their task easier (Berthier noted to Bourdessoulle that the Poles 'are impetuous, you should moderate their ardour'). Later they were also assigned light infantry, to offset the overwhelming numbers of Russian cossacks and light cavalry, and were issued better maps.

Less than a month into the campaign, the Grande Armée was suffering intensely. The pace of the advance was so fast that supply columns were left in the rear and the army was too large to live off a land virtually devoid of food and fodder. On 8 July General Preyssing saw General Pino's Italian division 'pass through the town [Sloboda] in very bad condition'. Maurice Tascher noted in his journal on 18 July: 'Retreated and camped in a village a mile to the rear. Hunger, extreme misery, suffering of the horses.' Two days later Emile Venturini complained in his journal that 'I ate some cabbage leaves and brought a sack of them back to my company and they devoured them avidly. We camped in the mud thanks to our two imbecile generals'. Less than a week later he added 'six men of our regiment died of hunger'. Even X Corps, a relatively small formation, needed 35,000 rations a day for the men and 8,000 for the horses and Lithuania was just incapable of providing sufficient food. Lithuanian recruits coming to join the regiments raised by the French were enlisted in early July and then disbanded for want of food. A Bavarian general noted to his king that 'catching sight of corpses each soldier recognised the fate awaiting him: to die of hunger'.

It wasn't just the want of food that was causing problems. Some 600 Bavarians had to be left at Glubkoi because they had no shoes. They were left in the charge of a Major Wattenbach although, presumably, he had retained his boots.

The hard marching, difficult weather and lack of resources caused the army's ranks to thin terribly by the end of July 1812. The Italian 2nd Line had counted 86 officers and 2,690 men on 25 June but by 3 August only 78 officers and 1,313 men were left. Statistics reported from the French hospital in Glubkoi on 27 July suggest that sickness was the prime cause of most of the Grande Armée's casualties thus far into the campaign; of 1,006 occupants 864 were suffering from 'fever', 110 had been wounded in battle, 14 had venereal disease and 18 were described as having scurvy. Being assigned to a hospital, rather than being left to die on the roadside, did not necessarily mean a passport to care and recovery. Hospitals established in the rear of the army soon received a notorious reputation on account of their squalor and filth. Montaigu wrote to Napoleon on 27 July, begging that more be done to ease the situation:

> The hospitals in Vilna are badly off and the number of sick has increased significantly recently. There are now at least 3,500 there. The town has provided nothing and the sick mostly lie on the stone floor of the hospital. Straw is impossible to find whilst some medicines have been issued, but only those purchased by the doctors themselves in the town.

Despite such problems, the pursuit of the Russians continued without relaxation. The Russians, now more confident in their movements since the departure of the Czar for St Petersburg on 16 July, did rally at Vitepsk towards the end of July, after shaking off the pursuing French cavalry at Ostrovno. They then withdrew, leaving the town to the French. Napoleon's troops thoroughly ransacked it for supplies, taking 500 bottles of wine from the Jesuit wine cellars. Some 10,000 lbs of coffee were also requisitioned from the town's shops. The Russians had resolved to concentrate at Smolensk and gave every sign that they intended to defend this ancient city with the combined armies of Barclay and Bagration. Their army had suffered considerably during its retreat from Vilna to Smolensk; some 30,000 men had disappeared from the ranks – some had been killed in battle, others had deserted, still more had fallen sick and been evacuated to hospital.

At Vitepsk, which went up in flames shortly after the arrival of the French, Napoleon, sensing the exhaustion of his own troops, and impending battle, allowed the forward elements of the French army a few days of much needed rest. A month of campaigning had not brought the decisive result Napoleon desired. Hoping that the Russians might now offer battle in defence of Smolensk he gathered his troops for the decisive clash and promised them winter quarters in the conquered city.

Napoleon advanced out of Vitepsk on the 14th, his cavalry encountering a division under Neverovskii and pushing it back after a bloody encounter. After a half-hearted celebration of the imperial birthday, Napoleon arrived outside the walls of Smolensk on the humid afternoon of 16 August. His army showed signs of the considerable stress and hardship it had undergone. Even so, the French were eager for battle and looked forward to contesting possession of Smolensk.

The Russians left a rearguard of 13,000 men under the determined Rayevski to defend the city and cover their withdrawal. The French and Russian armies fought a bloody battle on the evening of the 16th, and the Russians, now under Dokhturov, suffered heavily. Barclay, nervous at being cut off from the Moscow road, and fearing that a combined army of 105,000 men was insufficient to confront Napoleon's forces, had ordered the complete evacuation of the city that night. Bagration was despatched at dawn on the 17th to cover the Russian retreat eastwards and Barclay now determined to pull his entire command out of the city. The French launched a series of bloody assaults that day, supporting their attacks with massed artillery and setting the town on fire. Their troops pushed into the suburbs in the darkness, fighting a running battle, but their progress was arrested by the burning of the city's bridges. Meanwhile, the Russians evacuated Smolensk. The following morning, Ney's corps again bore the brunt of the French pursuit – the Württembergers once again finding themselves in the frontline – fighting a series of actions against Korf and Tutchkov. One such action at Valutina Gora developed into a determined fight, the French pouring in Gudin's division in support of Ney and the Russians bringing their artillery to bear. Unfortunately General Junot, commanding VIII Corps, coming up from the south, failed to exploit an opportunity to take the Russians in the rear and, towards nightfall on the 18th, the Russians disengaged and resumed their trek eastwards.

Smolensk, bombarded and consumed by countless fires, was a horror to behold. An officer of the Italian Guards of Honour described his regiment's entry into the city:

> Our musicians were placed at the head of the column and we marched in, passing ruin after ruin. Here the poor Russian wounded, covered in blood and gore, were sheltering. Many men had been asphyxiated and burnt and I saw wagons loaded with amputated limbs. French and allied soldiers were all that could be seen in the streets, hunting out whatever had been spared by the flames. We spent that night surrounded by ashes and bodies. The dying, the wounded, the living, men, women and children, filled the cathedral and whole families, tears in their eyes, fear and terror in their faces, sheltered in the aisles. Everyone trembled at our approach.

Ignoring his commanders' advice to halt and recover, and perhaps even winter at Smolensk, Napoleon still urged his troops forwards over the traditional boundary between Lithuania and Russia. The army was tense and there was still no sign of the victory that would decide the campaign.

The Russians too were nervous as they continued their retreat, and, after Smolensk, pressure mounted for Barclay to be replaced by a new commander, thus signalling an end to a frustrating withdrawal.

To the north Napoleon's Prussian allies, and a small Polish/German division, commanded by Marshal Macdonald, trundled over the Niemen, planning to lay siege to Riga. II and VI Corps, under Oudinot and St Cyr, marched roughly parallel with the Grande Armée's advance. In August they fought an indecisive battle with Wittgenstein's Russians at Polotsk. To the south the Austrians and Saxons of Schwartzenberg swept into the western Ukraine, playing cat and mouse with Tormassov's Russians.

Tormassov eagerly awaited news of the Russian Army of the Danube, 35,000 men under Admiral Chichagov, which was now marching northwards after Russia had hastily concluded peace with the Turks in May.

Napoleon's army continued to harry the Russians, Davout and Murat leading the advance. On the 29th the French received news that Barclay had been superseded by General Kutuzov. This, Napoleon believed, was a sure sign that the Russians would now offer battle. The crafty Kutuzov, popular with the Russian soldiers and the Russian nobility, had recently fought a successful campaign against the Turks and, although the Czar despised him, the old general was placed at the head of the Russian army and ordered to make a stand. Kutuzov sought hard for a suitable position to fight a defensive battle and eventually resolved to fight close to the little village of Borodino.

The Russians took up positions among the small hills and steep gullies that characterised the area. Their right flank was anchored on the river Kolotscha, their left protected by the thick forests around Utitza. To support their centre, placed largely on the heights to the south of Borodino village, the Russians built a series of earthworks bolstered by wood hewn from the foresty terrain – the most famous of which was dubbed the Grand Redoubt. Kutuzov had received reinforcements, mostly militiamen under Miloradovich and Markov, and believed that the governor of Moscow would be sending him more. In all, Russia deployed 120,000 men and 640 guns to bar Napoleon's way to Moscow.

Napoleon concentrated at Gjatsk. His troops advanced on the 4th, skirmishing constantly with the Russian rearguard. On the 5th, Murat felt his way along the Russian position and reported that the Russians were making a stand. That afternoon the French stormed Kutuzov's most advanced position – the Schevardino redoubt. Napoleon spent the next day on reconnaissance, hurrying forward as many troops as he could. By the evening of the 6th 128,000 French

Prince Eugene

and allies, with 580 guns, settled down before the Russian positions waiting for the order to attack. A Württemberg cavalry officer summed up the thoughts and fears of the entire French army:

We'd seen the Russian position and it was good, and we saw their entrenchments and, behind them, masses of troops, their weapons shining in the sun. We knew they had numerous artillery and that they would have made every effort to gather in as many troops as they could for the impending confrontation. The battle was sure to be tough, for both sides. We were convinced that our army was superior in number and that we were better acquainted with the practice of war. But we knew that the Russians were steady, and fought obstinately even against canister.

The French artillery began firing through the morning haze at 6 o'clock. Napoleonic warfare was a vicious affair, the resplendent uniforms notwithstanding. A Russian officer, Nikolai Andreyev of the 50th Jägers, on the receiving end of the bombardment, described the scene:

> During the night we had heard singing, drum rolls and military music coming from the enemy camp. At dawn we saw that a strong battery had been erected directly opposite our position. Something extraordinary then happened – as the guns opened up they made such a noise that they drowned out everything else. This lasted until midday. The smoke was such that it obscured the very sky. Our division was virtually destroyed by the artillery. I was sent back for ammunition, passing along a road choked with the dead and dying and too many horrors to describe. When I got back to Semenovskaya village I met Bourmine, our commander, at the head of forty men – all that remained of our regiment.

As the bombardment continued, Napoleon sent Ney, Davout and Eugene against the Russian positions whilst Prince Poniatowski and his Poles advanced against the Russian left. The advance in the centre and against Borodino degenerated into ferocious close-quarter fighting as both sides fed more and more men into the struggle. Shrouded in choking smoke, the battlefield was crowded with hundreds of small battles occasionally broken by a massed attack or a sudden withdrawal. Eugene's men took Borodino village and Ney managed to storm the fleches to the south of Semenovskaya village – only to lose them to a counter-attack by Bagavout.

Poniatowski's attack on the Russian left led to the Poles seizing Utitza but there were too few troops to make any further impression against Tutchkov. On the Russian right, Kutuzov agreed to send Platov and Uvarov on a flanking attack just as the French were absorbed by the drama around Borodino and the Grand Redoubt. The Russian horsemen were beaten off by Delzons' French and Croatian infantry, but not before sowing some apprehension and confusion on the French left. It was a key moment, the attack had alarmed Eugene and captured some baggage but, more importantly, had diverted attention from the centre.

As the Russian horsemen rode back to their lines, the French began to prepare a massive attack designed to break the Russian centre. Broussier's tired infantry and Caulaincourt's cavalry were ordered forwards. The Russians, exhausted and choked by the billowing smoke blowing into their faces, were sabred and bayoneted where they stood. Russian reserves counter-attacked with the bayonet but were mown down by the French artillery. As the Russians seemed at breaking point, with all their reserves committed, Napoleon was urged to consider an attack by his Imperial Guard – 25,000 fresh troops poised for victory. He decided against a final attack, claiming that he could not use his Guard so far from home, sent forward some horse artillery and directed his batteries to increase its fire and thus drive the Russians back. Late that evening, the Russians retreated to Mozhaisk, taking as many of their wounded as they could. Terrible night settled over the battlefield, the groaning of the wounded intermingled with distant explosions and alarms caused by cossack raiders. Heinrich von Brandt described the scene:

> In the shadows around each of our flickering fires, the agonised and tormented wounded began to gather until they far outnumbered us. They could be seen everywhere like ghostly shadows moving in the half-light, creeping towards the glow of the fire. Some, horrifically mutilated, used the last of their strength to do so. They would suddenly collapse and die, with their imploring eyes fixed on the flames.

Napoleon's army suffered 40,000 casualties (including 49 generals), whilst the Russians lost 47,000. For the French the experience of battle was demoralising. It had been a stubborn battle and merciless in the execution. Maurice Tascher's laconic journal summed up the experience:

> 7 September (Borodino): Mounted horses at 03.00. At 05.00 the first cannon shot is heard. At 07.00 we advance into range of the guns. The first redoubt falls. The army advances on the right. At 10.00 we take up another position by a ravine. At 12.00 we advance. At 15.00 we prepare to charge. Bourdonnais, etc., etc., wounded. Spend nine hours under fire. Sleep on the battlefield. Horrible night. Take water to wounded. Buried Russian emerges from ditch. The regiment had 280 men present of whom 97 were killed, wounded or dismounted including ten officers.

Leaving the Westphalians the harrowing task of burying the dead, Napoleon continued the advance towards Moscow, which was some 70 miles away. Covering this ground took the French a week. A fierce struggle for Mozhaisk, on the 9th, resulted in the French capture of that town, along with 10,000 unfortunate wounded Russians most of whom quickly died. On the 13th Kutuzov conferred with his generals and, contrary to their opinion that Moscow should not be given up without a further battle, put the welfare of his army first and avoided a further encounter by retreating towards Kaluga in the south, marching via Kolomna. It was the most testing part of the campaign for the Russians when Moscow was evacuated during the 13th and 14th. As the French arrived before the gates of the city they found it largely deserted, but for Russian wounded, prisoners released from the jails, foreign nationals and a handful of inhabitants.

Then, on the evening of the 15th, fires broke out throughout the city. It burned throughout that night and the following day. Moscow's wooden buildings were soon ablaze as the fire, fanned by strong winds, took hold. Not only did wooden buildings suffer, but out of 2,570 brick buildings only 578 survived the conflagration, the rest being completely gutted. Although some of the city remained untouched, including the Kremlin, most of Moscow was reduced to ashes. A quantity of supplies had been destroyed and, aside from alcohol and luxury goods, there was now a dearth of essentials – particularly forage for the horses.

Napoleon spent his time in Moscow dreaming up plans for possible offensives, reorganising his troops, directing Schwartzenberg's, Macdonald's and Victor's operations, sending a flurry of missives to Maret in Vilna, running the administration of his empire, reading novels, studying accounts of Pugachev's rebellion in the Ukraine, Karl von Plotho's book on the cossacks (published in 1811) and histories of Charles XII's invasion, and organising his temporary capital. As usual, he delighted in the details of running his army and empire and his correspondence varied from important matters of state in Spain to granting permission for a Danish sergeant-major in his army to return home on 11 October.

History does not record whether the Dane made it safely home but Albrecht Adam, who left Moscow before the retreat began, was fortunate to escape the fate of those who remained behind. Adam returned safely to Bavaria as recounted in his memoirs.

Napoleon's army had suffered appallingly as it trudged from Poland to Moscow. The heat, the rain, hunger and exhaustion had taken a terrible toll on the men who marched beneath his banners. Indeed the advance to Moscow was probably more of a disaster than the infamous retreat from Moscow that was to follow.

His army wasn't yet thinking of retreat as their most immediate concern was the hunt for food. Columns were despatched in the surrounding countryside when peasants failed to bring supplies to the reopened market. Food was collected by force of arms, which drove the peasants to take up arms or call in cossacks. The region collapsed into a shadowy war of partisans and desperate marauders.

Napoleon in 1812

Further to the west similar bodies of peasants and small units of cossacks or regulars began a war against Napoleon's endless line of communications. Convoys were attacked, cossacks pounced on small detachments, couriers were intercepted and isolated garrisons overwhelmed. Strict orders were issued for the movement of troops and strong punitive columns were dispatched from Smolensk and Moscow to keep the roads open and the army's crucial lifeline clear. That lifeline was also being menaced by the Russians coming up from the south under Chichagov and

pressure exerted by Wittgenstein from the north. Napoleon, aware of the growing number of seemingly unsolvable problems, sensing an impossible situation, strove hard to make Alexander negotiate, sending Lauriston to Kutuzov to present peace proposals. Alexander, determined as never before, refused to countenance peace with Napoleon. Lauriston was kept waiting before being sent back empty-handed. The army now began to talk of retreat. On the 14th orders were issued to stop artillery from proceeding beyond Smolensk. On the 16th preparations were made for the wounded to be evacuated from Moscow and orders were issued to the commissaries to gather stores of warm clothing in Smolensk. There was no talk of defeat, Napoleon writing to his Minister of Police in Paris that 'It is likely the war will be prolonged through the entire winter and only the occupation of St Petersburg will force Alexander to see the light. Moscow is no more.' All indications suggest that Napoleon was going to abandon Moscow towards the end of October; bad news, however, precipitated the departure.

Murat had shadowed Kutuzov's rearguard, fought in a number of small actions and then placed himself before the Russian's partially fortified camp at Tarutino. Here the Russian army received a steady stream of reinforcements and supplies and grew in strength and confidence throughout the first half of October. Despite an unofficial truce there was some skirmishing but, on 18 October, the Russians under Bennigsen launched an all-out attack, initially taking the French by surprise before being themselves driven back.

News of Tarutino arrived whilst Napoleon was reviewing III Corps. The Tarutino episode, and the loss of 36 guns, stung Napoleon into action. Leaving Mortier with a rearguard in the Kremlin – with orders to blow it up – the Grande Armée, followed by a huge caravan of vehicles and camp followers, marched off to the south-west in sombre procession. On 21 October the Kremlin was partially blown up and explosions continued until the 23rd.

The French marched towards Kaluga. An encounter battle flared up at Malojaroslavitz on the 23rd, Prince Eugene being attacked by Dokhturov and both sides feeding in reinforcements until the French and Italians drove the Russians, now under Kutuzov's own command, from the town. Kutuzov's Russians withdrew and took up a strong position two miles away, seemingly ready to fight every step of the way, but in fact themselves preparing to continue the withdrawal. Napoleon and his marshals, fearing another Borodino, altered course and marched for Mozhaisk and the old Moscow–Smolensk road. The retreat had begun.

This movement brought the French back into an area devastated by their own advance and the Russians' during the summer. Chaos and depression reigned in the French columns, which had stretched out along the road and covered 60 miles from vanguard to rearguard. Imperial orders to burn unnecessary waggons went largely unheeded and little attempt was made by officers to enforce the order as they themselves would be the ones losing out. The weather was still fine when, on 29 October, the French crossed over the morbid field of Borodino.

The Russian generals, sensing victory at last, but cautious in the presence of Napoleon's genius, sent cossacks forward to harass the French whilst their main body shadowed the enemy to the south-east. The cossacks took hundreds of prisoners and their mobile presence prevented the French from scavenging for food.

Then, to make matters worse, snow began to fall on 4 November. The French, and many of the Russians, found themselves unprepared. Their clothing was light and their horses were not shod for ice. Spirits dropped and casualties mounted in the French army. Wagons and guns were burnt or abandoned, troops threw down their weapons and the imperial army was increasingly shepherded along a road strewn with their own dead and dying.

Meanwhile, way to the south, the Russians under Chichagov and Sacken were eluding the Austrians and heading northwards. Wittgenstein, reinforced by troops from Finland, pushed against II and VI Corps on Napoleon's northern flank. An inconclusive battle was again fought at Polotsk on 19 October, but the French pulled back to Glubkoi (VI Corps), to cover Vilna, and Tchasniki (II Corps), to link up with Victor's IX Corps. The pressure was mounting and, on 7 November, a grave blow was struck when Vitepsk was captured by the Russians. Napoleon learned of this setback when, on 9 November he entered Smolensk with his Guard.

Smolensk was a ghostly city. There was little food and what was available was poorly distributed. Smolensk's administration had been sadly lacking and the reserves and reinforcements gathered there were totally dispirited by the appearance of the mass of fugitives that had once been the Grande Armée. It would have been impossible to winter in Smolensk now and so the retreat began again on the 12th, with Junot and the dismounted cavalry pushing ahead towards Orsha. Napoleon and the Guard left on the 14th, Eugene on the 15th. Davout – 'half-mad and good for nothing' according to Napoleon – and Ney, who was now acting as the rearguard, left on the 16th. The city's ramparts were blown up by the rearguard but the Russians instead of attacking Smolensk had skirted round the city and were preparing for another attempt to intercept the French. On 16th Miloradovich's men pounced near Krasnoi, cutting off Davout and Ney and bruising Eugene in the process. On the 17th, Napoleon turned back to assist Davout and Ney, who had still not left Smolensk. Davout slipped through the Russians, urging Ney forward, but III Corps, having found the Russians barring its way, turned into the woods and attempted to cross the Dnepr. After a series of running battles, characterised by desperate fighting in the incredible cold, Ney rejoined the army with just 500 men.

The dramatic escape of Ney, the bravest of the brave, did not raise morale in the French army for long as it staggered westwards. Any remaining hope was soon shattered by ugly rumours of the surrender of Minsk – a key French base, full of essential supplies – and the news that the Russians of Chichagov were advancing to cut the French line of retreat at the Beresina. The bridge at Borisov assumed tremendous importance, threatened now as it was by Russians advancing from the south and Wittgenstein's Russians pushing Victor down from the north. If the bridge could be cut then the French might be trapped. Napoleon was all too aware of the predicament and suspected that the bulk of his army was not fit for battle. Oudinot and Victor had arrived to swell the ranks of the force which had dragged its way back from Moscow. Lieutenant Begos, a Swiss officer in Oudinot's corps, described the effect of coming across the spectres from Moscow:

> It was indeed pitiful to see the remains of this once powerful army staggering back from Moscow, to all intents destroyed by battle, want and cold. I could not help but call to memory the fine troops who had left France, marched across Prussia and Poland and had been full of energy and buoyed by hope. We ourselves had suffered but we had arrived at the Beresina confident and full of fight. We had also managed to maintain some discipline and organisation and consequently were surrounded by the remnants of the army, oppressed by hunger, milling about seeking some solace for their woe.

Meanwhile, Chichagov had taken Minsk on 17 November and hurried northwards to the Beresina with his 35,000 veterans. On the 21st his vanguard defeated a weak French garrison commanded by Dombrowski defending the Borisov bridge. The Russians drove the French and Poles over the bridge and out through the little town of Borisov on the eastern bank. Oudinot counter-attacked and swept into the town but was unable to secure the bridge, which the Russians burned as they withdrew, severing the only viable bridge over the Beresina.

At Bobr news came to Napoleon that the Borisov bridge had been taken by Chichagov. On the morning of the 25th the emperor was told that the Borisov bridge had been destroyed but Oudinot then reported that his light cavalry, under Corbineau, had discovered a ford near Studianka and the marshal decided to use this ford as a crossing point, although the water was 1.5 metres deep and the river had widened due to a recent thaw. Napoleon despatched General Eblé and Chasseloup to aid Oudinot's artillery and engineers in constructing bridges. A detachment of Oudinot's troops made a demonstration to the south of Borisov, hoping to draw the Russians away from the scene of the impending action. To the surprise of all, the ruse worked and Chichagov, unaware of both Napoleon's and Kutuzov's armies, headed south leaving just Langeron opposite Borisov and a screen of cossacks opposite Studianka. The cossacks were soon cleared away by Corbineau's cavalry which swam across the river and Eblé could now throw himself into the task of constructing two bridges. Studianka was virtually demolished for wood and Eblé, who had destroyed the bridging train at Orsha saving only two wagons with essential tools, began work on the night of 25–26 November. His gallant bridging teams – some of whom were Dutch and some Sailors of the Imperial Guard – worked shoulder-deep in the freezing water. Napoleon was frequently down at the water's edge according to Lieutenant Begos:

> He lowered his head and then looked up and impatiently spoke to General Eblé:
> 'It's taking too long, general.'
> 'Sire, as you can see, my men are up to their necks in the water, the ice impairs their work and I have no food or brandy to revive them.'
> 'That will do,' said the emperor. He again looked at the ground and then, a few moments later, began to grumble again having now seemingly forgotten the general's words.

By noon the next day, two 100-metre-long bridges, one for infantry and cavalry and the other for vehicles and artillery, had been constructed. It had been a magnificent achievement.

Oudinot and Dombrowski were the first to cross and they secured a series of bridges which took the Vilna road over treacherous marshes around Zembin. As Oudinot was crossing the main army dragged its weary way from Borisov to the crossing point. Victor's three divisions of IX Corps took over rearguard duties from Davout and prepared to face Wittgenstein, and Platov and Yermolov who had been sent on ahead of Kutuzov's main army. The Russians were suffering too from lack of supplies and from the harsh weather. A German attached to the Russian staff comments:

> After Krasnoi our pursuit changed character. We could no longer march parallel to Napoleon's army but now had to follow the same route. Our situation was a little better than our adversary's, for we could rely on a certain level of supply. However, we were obliged to take up quarters in villages ruined and affected with typhus. The number of sick grew alarmingly and, despite our every effort, few of these unfortunates were ever to recover.

Throughout 27 November Ney and elements of the Young Guard crossed over to the right bank. Brandt, in Claparède's division, describes the crossing:

> It had stopped snowing, the cold had eased off slightly and it promised to be a fine day. It must have been around ten o'clock when our division, deployed in columns, began to cross the Beresina. The planks of the bridge were by no means even and when we crossed some of the planks were already missing, especially as we drew closer to the far bank. There the entire bridge was below the water-level and we had water up to our ankles.

With Victor's relatively fresh troops acting as rearguard, Napoleon sent his Guard over the river, followed by Junot, Eugene and Davout. The emperor himself crossed the Beresina, escorted by 200 Guard Chasseurs, later that afternoon. Between the units numbers of stragglers made their way over to the far side of the river even though Gendarmes were posted on the left bank to ensure only armed men were allowed across. A mass of weary stragglers had however encamped at the approaches to the bridge, blocking access and choking the movement of troops. They huddled around flickering campfires as the temperatures dropped. It was an exceptionally cold night.

As dawn broke Chichagov, realising his mistake, made his way northwards to Borisov and sent Langeron forwards. Langeron was beaten back by Ney, and Chichagov made preparations for an all-out attack.

At 9 a.m. the first wave of the Russian assault, consisting of seven regiments of Jägers supported by artillery, made its way forward through the snow and partially wooded and broken terrain, and opened a heavy fire on the French position. Oudinot's Swiss kept the Russians back by repeated bayonet charges until being forced back in turn by deadly Russian artillery. The French then launched a counter-attack spearheaded by Doumerc's cuirassier division and seized the initiative, launching an infantry attack in support. The Russians, unable to stand the pressure, were beaten back, thus allowing the Grande Armée to continue its march towards Vilna.

Whilst the bitter battle swung first this way and then that, the terrible ordeal of crossing the river continued. Jostled, crushed, pushed and shoved, crowds of fugitives streamed across the river, spurred on by panic and fear of Wittgenstein's guns – guns that were now in range of the bridges. For Victor was being steadily pushed back and lost his rearguard, commanded by Partonneaux, in confused fighting along the Borisov road. At 6 p.m., after it had already been dark for two hours, fighting died down before ceasing altogether.

That night, lit by a bright moon, Victor's corps began withdrawing, pushing its way towards the bridge and began crossing in good order at 9 p.m.. The last formed troops to cross were von Zech's Baden grenadiers, marching over at 1 p.m.. They left 20,000 stragglers huddled around the flickering fires; worn out and inert they awaited the morning.

Eblé had orders to destroy the bridges the next morning but he delayed as long as possible to give the non-combatants a final chance to cross. Then, being unable to risk the bridges falling into Russian hands, he ordered Seruzier to fire them at 9 a.m.. An anguished howl arose as their only means of escape went up in flames. The majority would perish of hunger or of cold, but a vast number would die of typhus, which swept the little town of Borisov over the next few weeks.

A Russian officer described the appalling scene at the foot of the fatal bridges:

> Nothing in the world more saddening or distressing. One saw heaped bodies of men, women and even children; soldiers of all arms, all nations, choked by the fugitives or hit by our artillery; horses, carriages, guns, ammunition wagons, abandoned carts. One cannot imagine a more terrifying sight than that of the two broken bridges, and the river frozen to its very bottom. Both sides of the road were piled with dead in all positions, or with men dying of cold, hunger exhaustion, their uniforms in tatters, and beseeching us to take them prisoner. However much we might have wished to help, unfortunately we could do nothing.

The French, turning their backs on the disaster, pressed on towards Vilna. The cold had grown more intense, morale and discipline had collapsed altogether. The instinct for self-preservation, in all its brute selfishness, now, more than ever, came to the fore. Many participants described unfortunates being knocked to the ground, stripped, pillaged and left to die. Thousands marched past men imploring help, begging for food or lying slumped around half-extinguished fires. For Maurice Tascher, struggling along with his brother Eugene, this was the hardest part of the retreat:

> 4 December: Bitter cold. Silence. Much thinking. My birthday. Remember my mother. Tears. Agony. Did 18 miles. Lodged in a village two miles from HQ. Fever and diarrhoea. Eugene suffers horribly.

Reserves sent out to support the Grande Armée, such as Loison's youthful division, quickly dissolved, reduced to as miserable a state as the Moscow army in a matter of days. The rearguard, under Ney, pressed by the Russians, surrounded by starving stragglers and fugitives and marching along a route already stripped of food and shelter, fought a series of desperate actions between the Beresina and Vilna and preserved what it could of the Grande Armée's honour.

All eyes looked to Vilna for respite. Every eyewitness account makes it clear that Vilna was akin to the Promised Land where food, warmth and shelter would be found and all the trouble and misery would be left behind. But before it was reached, Napoleon quit his army. He would head for Paris to prepare for the next campaign, negate the impact of bad news from the east and rouse his tardy government. Command of the army passed to Murat and it was the cavalryman that led what little remained of the army into a surprised Vilna on 9 December. The Lithuanian capital had pursued the life of a normal garrison town between June and December. It was unprepared for the visitation unleashed upon it in early December. Socrate Blanc, an assistant surgeon, had been based there, had his portrait painted by a Dutch artist, and complained about nothing more than the exorbitant prices in the city's restaurants. François-Joseph Bailly, a pharmacist with the Imperial Guard, had also been left behind at Vilna because of his weak chest and he painted a vivid picture of the sudden arrival of the great army from Moscow. The population had heartily celebrated the anniversary of the coronation of Napoleon on 2 December. On 3 December rumours were circulating that the French had been defeated on the Kaluga road after Moscow had been evacuated. On 7 December word reached the city of the battle at Krasnoi and that the emperor was nearing the city. Then, on 8 December, at the Saint Basil gate, the Grande Armée began to trickle into the city:

> On the first day it was infantry and dismounted cavalry, sick and the wounded, and these were directed into the city's hospitals. When asked about news of the army, they replied that it was in Smolensk but that headquarters was to be at Vilna. They themselves had been evacuated to the capital of Lithuania as the reserve was to be organised here. On the second day a horde of stragglers arrived on foot or mounted, pretending that their units were just behind them and that these would show up the following day. But, on 9 December, it was a defeated army which arrived: officers, soldiers, infantry, cavalry, artillery, all mixed together without weapons and dressed in whatever they had been able to lay their hands on to protect themselves from the cold. These men, who had escaped from the Beresina, took refuge in the hospitals or in private houses, dying of cold and hunger. Most died shortly after receiving some aid.

Vilna could not cope with the desperate influx and was simply overwhelmed. Rations had been gathered through heavy and burdensome requisitions across Lithuania and there was sufficient food for 100,000 men for 40 days in the city's storehouses. But, thanks to looting and hopeless distribution, too few troops got too little food. Murat found new responsibility intolerable and it became apparent that, contrary to Napoleon's expectations, he

Murat

did not wish and was not able to hold the city. The despondent French abandoned Vilna on the 10th, dragging themselves free from the exhausted Russian pursuit. They sent mostly cossacks against the French, for their line units were feeling the rigours of the climate and were exhausted by continual movement.

As the French abandoned Vilna, hasty orders went out to Macdonald and Schwartzenberg to pull back over the Niemen, something the main body did on the 13th, passing through Kovno and crossing the Russian frontier into the Grand Duchy of Warsaw.

As Macdonald was withdrawing, his Prussian contingent hesitated and was overtaken by the Russians. The Prussians quickly signed a convention, which effectively made it clear that their divisions had defected.

Murat, learning of the convention, appointed Eugene commander of the army and withdrew to Naples. Eugene threw most of the survivors into fortresses along the Vistula. Most of these would be besieged the next year, their garrisons either dying from disease or surrendering to the victorious Allies. Others were called upon to serve as cadres for the new army that was being raised by Napoleon, an army that would fight in Germany in 1813 and would, for the most part, perish in an equally futile endeavour.

As the remains of the army staggered back into Prussia and Poland the full scale of the disaster began to emerge. Many of those who made it into Germany did not survive long. Maurice Tascher died of sickness in January 1813 as did General Eblé, hero of the Beresina. Some were more fortunate. Emile Venturini had been wounded on 18 October at Polotsk but he was carried to Vilna on the back of a horse, had nothing to eat and almost froze on the journey. Placed in a hospital he was barely encouraged by a doctor who declared 'if this one does not die there is hope for the others'. Only able to walk using crutches, he left Vilna on 1 December in a carriage owned by some Swiss officers although they spent much of their time running to keep warm. Finally, Venturini made it into Germany to find that his regiment had virtually disappeared.

Casualties had indeed been horrific. Eugene was able to gather some 30,000 survivors, some 10,000 were thrown into Danzig, and perhaps 60,000 (largely unreliable) Austrians, Poles and Saxons remained to cover Warsaw. This, and the few thousands wounded and sick that had been evacuated during the campaign, was all that remained of both the mighty host that had crossed the Niemen and the troops subsequently despatched in support. Of course many thousands had deserted, and made their way quietly back to their homelands but, even so, the vast majority had perished or fallen into the hands of the Russians. I, II, III and IV Corps combined numbered just 6,400 infantry in February 1813. The Old Guard could field just 500, with another 800 in

hospital. Individual regiments had ceased to exist – the 6th Voltigeurs and 6th Tirailleurs of the Young Guard were reported as having no survivors in February 1813 – or were so reduced as to be disregarded as units. The 4th Line (III Corps) had just 102 survivors out of the 2,300 men that had marched into Russia; the 53rd Line reported just 52.

The cavalry seems to have suffered even more. The 11th Hussars had 65 officers and men present in early 1813, Saxony's Garde du Korps just 26. Napoleon's allies and vassals had suffered tremendously, even those that had not gone as far as Moscow. The Bavarian VI Corps crossed the Niemen back into Poland some 300 men strong, having lost 28,700 men in the course of the campaign. Eugene's Italians had suffered particularly badly. Even though the four Italian infantry regiments, serving as part of IV Corps, had not fought at Borodino, they counted just 70 officers and men in December 1812, the demoralised survivors of nearly 10,000 fine troops (for example the unfortunate Italian 2nd Line had counted 86 officers and 2,690 men on 25 June 1812 but on 24 December 1812 had just 14 officers and four men present under arms). Eugene's Royal Guard, soldiers of which feature in many of Adam's plates, was nearly destroyed. By 24 December 1812 the Guard Infantry Regiment had been reduced to 28 officers and 47 men. By 7 January there were just 12 officers and four men left. The impressive Guards of Honour emerged from Russia with just three officers and 31 men. Perhaps more were in hospital but many more lay on the fields and roads of Russia.

Although a number of deserters, stragglers and sick later rejoined the remnants of the Grande Armée, it is estimated that the French lost nearly 450,000 soldiers, killed or made prisoner during the campaign. This astonishing figure includes some civilian camp followers and refugees from Moscow, but by no means all. Some 175,000 French army horses were also lost, along with nearly 1,500 guns and hundreds of waggons. Between 1813 and peace in May 1814 the Russians released 100,000 prisoners of war, a few thousand stayed on in Russia, having been offered citizenship, a place in the ranks of the Russo-German Legion or, like Dr Roos or the Frenchman who became lecturer in French Literature at Kharkhov University, regular, peaceful employment.

Russian losses had been enormous. Some 250,000 regular troops had perished or gone missing, and tens of thousands were crippled or maimed. Thousands of peasants had perished. Every town and almost every village along the French line of march was in ruins. Moscow, Smolensk, Vitepsk and countless other towns had been utterly destroyed. Russia was marred by smoking ruins and heaps of rotting corpses. As winter turned to spring, epidemics began to break out along the route where the French army had retreated and added to the death toll.

Napoleon's campaign in Russia is characterised by its massive toll on human life. Behind the statistics lurk hundreds of thousands of individual stories of death, starvation and destruction. In an era when armies did not communicate casualties to officers' families, let alone soldiers' families, most of Napoleon's Grande Armée almost literally disappeared in Russia. So we have Socrate Blanc, a 19-year-old assistant surgeon working in Vilna who simply vanished and his family never heard of him again. Or we have cases such as the Flamant family of Strasbourg. René Flamant's son, Pierre Flamant, was serving with the 129th Line Regiment in 1812. On 22 February 1813, having heard no news, René wrote the following letter to his son assuming he was a prisoner at Vilna:

We have had no news from you, my dear Flamant. Your last letter is dated 29 August. Since then I have only heard about you indirectly. I like to think that you are a prisoner and that is the only consolation we have at the moment. Your poor mother is sick with worry and a single word from you would restore her to health. If this letter reaches you it will tell you that we are alive and have no other desire than to see you or at least to learn that you still live. You might be wanting for everything but you should know that my purse is as open as my heart. Write to us and just ask. We have the means to send you assistance.

Your mother, your brother, your sisters and I await the moment when we can embrace you. Your father and friend, R. Flamant.

But Pierre Flamant was not at Vilna. He had been wounded on 5 December 1812 and had disappeared before reaching that city. He was never seen again.

On the Russian side it was a similar story. Peasants abandoned their homes and died miserable deaths in frosty forests only to be buried anonymously in mass graves. Empires come crashing down and beneath the dry accounts of historical facts lie hidden individual tragedies.

The Russian army, now much reduced and fatigued, arrived on the Niemen in January 1813. Despite Kutuzov's reluctance, the Russians crossed over the river and took the war into Poland and Prussia. Sweden came out in open support of Russia on 7 January and, on 27 February 1813, Prussia too declared war, a veritable war of liberation, on France.

Napoleon, back in Paris, feverishly tried to raise another army to stem the all-conquering Allies. But it was not the same army as the force he had marched into Russia and inevitably Germany was quickly cleared of imperial troops. Then invasion came to France and Paris would soon see cossacks trotting down the boulevards.

Six months in 1812 was all it took to decide the fate of Europe. In June 1812 Napoleon was at the height of his power, he was master of a powerful empire. By December he had lost an army and his hold on his dominions was fatally diminished. Defeat in Russia began a sequence of events which would lead to Allied troops marching in triumph through Paris and to Napoleon being exiled from the continent of Europe. Defeat in Russia ushered in Napoleon's fall.

10 June 1812

Willenberg, Headquarters

At that time the pretty little east Prussian town of Willenberg was flooded with soldiers. The poor inhabitants, who bore their lot with considerable patience despite the tribulations of war, doubtless later recalled these times with horror. The Viceroy was accommodated a little distance from this house in a little country mansion. This is the first picture I sketched and it was here I made the first entry in my journal.

Plate 1

10 June 1812

Camp of the Italian Guard Dragoons Near Willenberg

The Viceroy had personally solicited orders from the Emperor and, upon his return, all the necessary preparations were completed to get the troops moving. The corps began to march on 4 June and reached Soldau on the 6th. Here they were granted a rest whilst ovens were constructed, so essential for the feeding of the troops. We then set off for Willenberg where the troops were again granted a 48-hour rest.

It was at Willenberg that I joined the army and here is my first study of troops from that army – a scene from the camp of some Italian Guards.

Plate 2

13 June 1812

Sensbourg, Headquarters

Sensbourg is a little town in eastern Prussia but it didn't provide much by way of accommodation. It was, however, somewhat distinguished by its architecture, its people, the fact that it was to be the last German town we marched through and for the role it had played in previous campaigns. However bad our billets seemed we should have been lucky had they been as good during the rest of our march on Moscow.

This scene is set in the market place of the little town. Chaos rules. French and Italian soldiers from all branches of service are all mixed up with wagons carrying forage and flour, carts belonging to commissaries, bakers or grocers, the household wagons of the Viceroy, sutlers' vehicles, Italian Guards and those conducting herds of livestock. Everyone was hunting out somewhere to stay, looking for good shelter or any shelter.

It was here, though, that we began our catastrophe. Such privations were to be met that here we could only guess at. This was not to be war as war had previously been. Those successful campaigns now came to an end.

Plate 3

14 June 1812

Rastenbourg, Headquarters

After three days' march we arrived in Rastenbourg, a pretty little place surrounded by lakes. Here we found supplies and we encountered more people than ever since we had quit Glogau. This picture represents the place in the town at which the Viceroy was lodged. His horses are in front of the building as is a squad of Italian Guards ready for departure.

Plate 4

24 June 1812

Kalvary

The Viceroy's corps arrived in Kalvary in absolutely splendid weather, it was an excellent time of year. Here, too, there was sufficient food and the troops camped in some comfort. The Viceroy was accommodated in a little chateau, his officers were scattered about in the vicinity, for the most part being housed in poor and dirty huts inhabited by Jews.

Here we see a group of Italian Guards of Honour. These men were drawn from the best Italian families and were quite accustomed to the finer things in life. Here they are sitting on their beds of straw partaking of their frugal meal. Generally speaking you could count yourself lucky if you found a roof below which you might shelter. In this campaign most nights were spent beneath the stars, at the mercy of the cold nights, the wind and the rain.

Plate 5

26 June 1812

Italian Guards of Honour, Marienpol

In this place, of no geographical or military significance, I took the opportunity of drawing a number of sketches. I chose this group of Italian Guards of Honour for the subject of one such study. Here we see a group of soldiers preparing to camp.

Some of the men, wearing their campaign uniform, are preparing the meal. Two of the Guards, in full uniform, have, however, just come off duty. This unit, composed of the sons of well-to-do Italian families, was in excellent spirits despite all the forced marches and the readily apparent contrast between the climate here and that which they enjoyed in their native land.

Plate 6

27 June 1812

Italian Guards of Honour, Michalsky

A terrible storm raged as the Italian Guards of Honour struggled hard to build their camp. This was to be near Michalsky, a small place surrounded by forests. But there was a complete lack of almost everything, even dry wood for fuel. And fires were so important if you were to spend such cold nights beneath the stars.

The Viceroy maintained the strictest of discipline in his corps and good order was maintained. Nobody dared enter the grounds of houses without his permission and this could only be obtained by addressing to him a list of pressing needs.

Unfortunately, two soldiers of the Guard began a quarrel about these orders. The hot blood of these two Italians was barely cooled by the pouring rain, indeed the argument became so violent that both reached for their swords. The following morning one of the soldiers was stretched out dead in the field.

Plate 7

29 June 1812

Near Pilony, by the Niemen

The Viceroy's quarters were located in this appalling village. We were all lodged in horrible huts, barely sheltered from the insults of the weather. Food was now scarce and the rain fell in torrents, drenching the men and the horses. Deprived of adequate shelter, the former made the best of the situation but the latter, weakened by their exertions on impassable roads, succumbed in droves. They collapsed in their hundreds by our camp. Alongside the roads, in the fields, there were piles of dead horses and hundreds of abandoned carts and the scattered contents of the baggage trains.

In July we felt the cold, the rain and the pangs of want. Because of the lack of forage the horses were being fed on green corn, trampled down by the rain. The poor creatures ate their fill but, shortly afterwards, collapsed dead. I have tried to capture this morbid scene in the plate opposite.

Plate 8

30 June 1812

The Viceroy's Headquarters at Pilony

Pilony was rendered infamous by its destitution and the terrible conditions there. Here we see the Viceroy's domestics preparing his meal. It was here that the army found itself deprived of even the basic necessities. There was no shelter from the freezing rain which fell without interval for two days. This deluge soaked everyone and wet even our change of clothing in our bags and portmanteaux. It was also impossible to warm oneself and this struggle against the damp cold impressed itself upon everyone who took part in this testing campaign.

Plate 9

30 June 1812

Crossing the Niemen

It was on this day that Delzons' 13th and Broussier's 14th divisions crossed the Niemen unopposed. The Italian Guard, commanded by General Lecchi, crossed on the 1st followed by Pino's division. The Italians crossed the river under the gaze of their Viceroy and there were spontaneous shouts of enthusiasm. The Viceroy was flattered by this honour, rendered to him by well-turned-out and disciplined troops more than 600 leagues from home, and expressed his satisfaction to them.

Plate 10

1 July 1812

Kroni, Headquarters

No sooner had we crossed the river than we seemed to exist in another atmosphere. The roads were as bad as they had been, the forests just as sad and the villages even more deserted, but we, animated by the imagination of conquerors, beheld everything with enchantment.

After a two-hour march across muddy terrain we arrived at the village of Kroni with its wooden chateau and houses. That might be the last time I make such an observation because all Russian villages were so constructed. We found brandy in the village and the soldiers pillaged it with avidity. As there were no Jews here, the place was deserted and this fact made us realise that the enemy were intent on creating a desert of the region we were passing through – man and beast had been evacuated.

Plate 11

3 July 1812

Riconti, near Vilna

A campsite occasionally offered a view which might make one forget all the martial sites scattered around. Such was the case at Riconti, itself a miserable little village, where we arrived one afternoon in marvellous weather. The Viceroy's tent was fixed on some high ground which afforded a splendid view over the surrounding countryside and over a small lake which reflected the dying sun's rays. On the shore of the lake was a camp erected and abandoned by the Russians. Our own camp was some little way off and a sublime silence reigned around us. I made the most of such an opportunity and, with my sketch pad beneath my arm, I sallied forth to find the most appealing view. Thus it was that I came across the place where the Viceroy, our venerable commander, lay asleep covered by a white sheet. One of his aides-de-camp, General Triaire, kept watch and made sure nothing disturbed him. Nevertheless the Viceroy's sleep was soon disturbed and this reminded us that in this base profession of arms, the greatest captain and the simple soldier shall be deprived of even an hour's repose. An officer, bearing an order from the emperor approached the slumbering prince. What should he do? The emperor's orders took precedence and it was, indeed, a rude awakening.

The emperor's despatch destroyed our hope of marching into Vilna, our much-longed for destination. Instead we were ordered to make for Vitepsk and not set foot in a town which could have alleviated our suffering. So it was that IV Corps, with loud complaint, formed up and marched around the capital of Lithuania.

Plate 12

3 July 1812

Imperial Guardsmen near Vilna

This image represents a scene which I observed near our camp in the environs of Vilna and I think it's a worthy study. A dragoon, belonging to the Imperial Guard, lies next to two elite grenadiers who are resting after undertaking another difficult march. They seem absorbed by serious reflections or perhaps they suspect that it is a sinister fate that awaits them.

Plate 13

4 July 1812

Trokiy, Headquarters

After a four-hour journey through woods and forests we arrived at Nev-Trokiy, a place perched on some heights and surrounded by lakes. It was an attractive place and it was a true contrast to the terrain we had just traversed. Everyone was astonished by the appearance of the town, in particular a huge convent on the summit of the mountain dominating the town. Others were struck by the fine forests or the water which, apparently, never froze. Anyone with an artistic eye could not fail to admire such attractive scenery. In the middle of one of the lakes was a ruined castle with tumbledown walls which was both reflected on the lake and jutted up into the vermilion sky. Trokiy was an enchanted place, or so it seemed. But the spell was shattered as soon as we set foot in the town. As we approached the outlying houses, a troop of Jews emerged, accompanied by women, children and the infirm. They fell at our feet, imploring us to deliver them from the rapacity of the soldiers who had burst into the houses and were busy carrying off or destroying whatever they could lay their hands on. We, alas, could do very little but offer them empty consolation. There were no stores as such in the town and our troops, deprived of rations, now lived off the land. Indeed, this was the beginning of that fatal indiscipline, with all its odious consequences, which marked the demise of our army.

Plate 14

Night of 8 to 9 July 1812

The Viceroy of Italy's Camp, Wielke-Solezniki

On the 8th we were hit by such a terrible storm that the Viceroy and his entire staff were obliged to call a halt to their march along the main road even though they were but three miles from Imperial Headquarters. They did this in an attempt to escape the torrential rain. Horses could make no further progress and anyone attempting to ride soon ground to a halt. Eventually, the march was resumed and we arrived at Headquarters soaked to the skin and absolutely exhausted. Fortunately, a beautiful summer's evening gave us respite and this probably persuaded the Viceroy to sleep beneath the stars rather than risk a night in a dirty house prey to vermin.

One of the Prince's aides-de-camp, General Triaire, lies next to him on a simple wooden bed with a mattress of straw. A soldier from the Guards of Honour stands sentinel next to the fire.

Plate 15

11 July 1812

In the Courtyard of Holzany Castle, Headquarters of the Viceroy of Italy

The Viceroy's headquarters were located in the ancient castle of Holzany for the night of 11 to 12 July and I thought the castle's courtyard would make a fitting subject for a painting. This was particularly true as such buildings are relatively rare in this region.

The castle walls ring living quarters inhabited by an old landowner. The grounds boast a pretty garden, laid out in the English style, and the castle's estates are fertile and lush. There was also a stud farm, boasting excellent Polish stock, and all of this announced to the world the wealth and comfort of the landowner.

Plate 16

16 July 1812

General Pino's Division on the March

Despite the Viceroy's every effort to preserve order in his corps, and to seek to maintain the troops well fed and in condition, there were many soldiers who, as they marched through the deserts of Lithuania, were subject to the most cruel privations. The burden of want fell, in particular, on Pino's division as this unit was acting as rearguard. There was no lack of meat but the scarcity of bread was greatly felt. Soldiers were soon reduced to such a state that you could see them literally collapse by the roadside unable to continue despite their every effort.

One evening as we trotted alongside a column of Italians dragging itself along, we saw one such unfortunate collapse into the dusty sands of the road. A grenadier, who had been marching next to him, vainly sought to persuade his comrade to move. Finally, an officer, mounted on a poor pony, arrived and convinced the man to march on to the next shelter. Taking the soldier's haversack, and that of the grenadier, he trotted on whilst the grenadier, carrying his musket as well as his own, supported his exhausted comrade. The two of them staggered on as the column continued its lugubrious march.

I could not resist sketching such a moving scene.

Plate 17

A Study of Some French Soldiers

My aim was to include images of picturesque scenes alongside images of martial or historic events. Nevertheless I could not resist including some images which, by virtue of the pleasure they might afford to those who also practise the profession of artist, seemed particularly apt. Such interesting scenes were relatively common. This image shows a group of French soldiers slumped on the banks of the Niemen.

The soldiers belong to the French infantry whilst the officer is a Guard horse artillery officer.

Plate 18

18 July 1812

Dokzice

We set off for Dokzice, a march of 21 miles being necessary to reach that place. The town is inhabited almost exclusively by Jews. It has an attractive central square, a church and a miserable mansion house constructed of wood. The outskirts of the town are built on two heights with a little marshy stream running through the middle. On the day we actually spent in the town the Viceroy was accommodated in the mansion house. A small plume of smoke was spied rising from just behind this place, quickly followed by flames. Soon the fire was consuming the neighbouring houses but, fortunately, the army rushed to our assistance and our fears vanished when the fire subsided.

Plate 19

21 July 1812

A Russian Prisoner of War at Headquarters, Kamen

On 22 July one of our chasseurs, serving on the picquets, brought a Russian prisoner back with him to headquarters. This man, by his singular conduct, attracted universal attention. He seemed so familiar with the men of our advanced posts that he had been eating and drinking with them. Even before the Prince, who wished to speak with him, his conduct showed such pluck as almost bordered on temerity.

The following day we heard that he had been granted a little freedom in his movements and, taking advantage of that, he had absconded during the night without anyone being aware of how or when. This gave rise to much conjecture and I won't repeat that here as the truth was never arrived at.

The man next to the prisoner in this plate is the Prince's Mameluke who had accompanied the Viceroy since the Egyptian expedition but who, alas, came to an untimely end.

During the retreat the Mameluke was taken seriously ill and stayed behind at Kovno. His master left him a sum of money and entrusted him to the care of some charitable individuals, but he was never heard of again. There were accusations that the man had simply given up and that he should have made every effort to keep up with the army. But, for my part, I believe that the suffering he endured personally, and witnessing that of the persons closest to him, broke his body and his soul. Frank, sincere, loyal and courageous, he showed that he was more than a servant and that such a master was worthy to have such an assistant.

I was a personal friend of the man and it is with great pleasure that I conserve for posterity the memory of him by this faithful portrait.

Plate 20

21 July 1812

Bezenkovitschi

After crossing a little river, known as the Svetscha, our troops found themselves in Bezenkovitschi. In fact the town was already full of troops as Bruyeres' and Saint-Germain's cavalry division had arrived in the place having come from Oula. However, such a large concentration of troops, destined for Vitepsk, did not intimidate the enemy who, on the far side of the Dvina, manoeuvred his cavalry and fired on our voltigeurs who were endeavouring to get over the river and seize the ferry.

The Viceroy determined that it might be possible to force a passage over the river and had two guns brought up to protect a party of sappers charged with building a pontoon bridge. Meanwhile, however, the Sailors of the Royal Guard, commanded by Captain Tempié, moved forwards. These brave men, encouraged by the presence of their Prince, threw themselves into the water and, despite the enemy's fire, headed for the ferry. Our guns, and some of our skirmishers who now opened up some covering fire, convinced the Russians to evacuate the far bank and we were able to retrieve the ferry whilst the sappers finished their bridge.

Plate 21

24 July 1812

Crossing the Dvina near Bezenkovitschi

The Bavarian cavalry, commanded by general Preyssing, particularly distinguished itself during the crossing of this river. General Preyssing's cavalry division managed to locate a ford a few hundred paces downstream from the bridge which was thrown over the Dvina. After having crossed the river, the cavalry found themselves supported by a few companies of infantry who had made the crossing on the ferry. The troops advanced, pushing before them an enemy bent on flight. We greatly admired the conduct of the Bavarians with their precise movements and the excellent way in which they were commanded. They were held as role models by anyone who knew anything about the art of war.

Plate 22

24 July 1812

Napoleon Reconnoitres the Right Bank of the Dvina

We were busy watching the Bavarian manoeuvres when word came that the Emperor was about to arrive. The first courier bearing this news was quickly followed by a second confirming the news. Soon a body of horsemen came into sight and the town played host to staff officers and generals of the guard even though it was already full to bursting. Napoleon appeared in the midst of the tumult. Making his way through the town square he headed for the river bank to the point where the bridge had been built. In a rather dry and humourless tone he found fault with its construction. Nevertheless, he mounted his horse and rode over it, joining up with the Bavarian cavalry on the plain on the far side of the river. He accompanied them for some distance before turning around and returning to the town.

Plate 23

25 July 1812

On the Road from Bezenkovitschi to Ostrovno

The Viceroy had sent ahead his personal baggage escorted only by a picquet of dragoons so that his lodgings in a small manor house on the roadside could be arranged. Some cossacks on the far side of a river were skitting about and the dragoons amused themselves by shouting out 'come and get us'. Such pleasantries ceased however when the Russians unmasked a battery they had concealed in a small wood. Their fire was so accurate that in no time at all the manor house had been hastily evacuated. Everyone ran for it or sought to get the horses and wagons out of danger. Soon skirmishers moved up and a warm exchange of fire eventually cleared the far bank of the enemy. A few horses belonging to the escort were wounded. The Viceroy, arriving a while later, spent little time here before pressing on to Ostrovno where a serious battle had flared up when Murat's cavalry had encountered the Russians.

Plate 24

25 July 1812

Near Bezenkovitschi

Our troops were ordered to advance on Ostrovno and our staff were on the way there when we heard a massive artillery barrage. Shortly afterwards, one of General Delzons' aides came galloping up and announced to the Viceroy that our troops had encountered the enemy near that town and that a fierce struggle now ensued. No sooner had the aide finished speaking than the noise of the bombardment intensified. The Viceroy ordered the baggage to halt and, followed by just his senior officers, he headed for Ostrovno to join up with the King of Naples. He had Bruyeres' and Saint-Germain's cavalry divisions with him as well as the infantry of the 13th Division.

Plate 25

25 July 1812

The Battle of Ostrovno

Murat was marching on Ostrovno with his cavalry, Domon, du Coetlosquet, Carignan and the 8th Hussars, when they, advancing in column along the wide road, came to a hill some six miles from that place. Climbing the slope, they had just reached the summit when they spied three regiments of Russian Guard Cavalry and six guns. No skirmishers covered the Russian line.

The 8th Hussars thought themselves supported by two further regiments from their division and thought that the trees on either side of the road merely hid these supports from their view. But, in fact, these regiments had halted and the 8th was now well ahead of them. The sudden appearance of the Russians surprised the officers of the 8th so they sent one of their number ahead to ascertain what troops were positioned before them. Suddenly he was sabred, knocked off his horse and seized. Then the Russian guns opened up. The 8th, without losing a minute more, resolved to charge. Their impetuous attack overran the Russian guns and overwhelmed the regiment stationed in the Russian centre. In the tumult caused by their initial success, they realised that the Russian regiment on the right stood transfixed with amazement so they wheeled about and took the Russians in the rear. With this second victory almost achieved, the third Russian regiment, disconcerted, now sought to retire but the Hussars fell on this regiment too and dispersed it.

At Ostrovno our forces took a number of cannon and ammunition wagons as well as seizing numerous prisoners. Most of these belonged to the Dragoons and Cossacks of the Russian Imperial Guard. As well as the dead which littered the battlefield the area around about was covered with baggage, munitions and weapons as well as countless dead horses.

Flushed with success, Murat sought to press on into the Ostrovno woods but soon a more stubborn resistance obliged him to halt.

Plate 26

26 July 1812

The Battle of Ostrovno

Prince Eugene reached Ostrovno at around three in the morning. IV Corps camped around him whilst the cavalry, some way off to the front, watched the enemy closely.

At six in the morning the Viceroy and the King rode out to the front line, crossing the field of yesterday's battle. As they moved forwards they received reports that Osterman's corps had been reinforced by Kanovitzen's division. So it was that the Viceroy ordered his infantry to support the King of Naples' cavalry. The Hussars, sent forward to scout, had penetrated into the woods but sent word back that the Russians seemed determined to resist any further advance. And indeed the air was filled with the noise of skirmishing whilst the Russian cannon pounded our columns as they marched forwards along the main road.

Plate 27

Noon, 26 July 1812

The Battle of Ostrovno

With some progress being evident on the left and in the centre, the King of Naples and the Viceroy rode over to the right wing and urged it to come into action. The Russians, positioned in the woods, were fighting tenaciously and were keeping the 92nd Line Regiment at bay. This regiment, even though it was placed on some heights, was obliged to halt. Seeing this the Viceroy sent Adjudant Forestier to lead the regiment forwards but progress was slow and the Duke d'Abrantes, impetuous as ever, dashed forwards to rally the men. Electrified by his presence, or rather his example, the 92nd, with General Rousel at their head, charged forwards and burst into the woods to do battle with our courageous enemy.

On our extreme right a Russian column attempted to outflank us but, realising the danger, quickly sought to fall back. Spying this column, Murat rode over to his cavalry and ordered them to fly at the column, cut its retreat and urge it to lay down its arms. The difficult terrain obliged a slight delay in the cavalry's movement and Murat, who wanted the action to be as quick as the thought, dashed ahead shouting out that the brave should follow him. We were filled with admiration by this heroic deed and each sought to follow the King. We would have made the column prisoners had some deep ravines not slowed us down. The Russian column soon joined up with the main body of troops from which it had been detached.

Plate 28

Afternoon of 26 July 1812

The Battle of Ostrovno

Whilst we moved to attack on the left, the Russians sought to attack our right. Seeing this, the Viceroy sent the 13th Division in support and Russian progress was soon halted.

Our artillery, placed as it was on some low heights, soon began to reassure us that our line would not be broken by an enemy assault.

Plate 29

Afternoon of 26 July 1812

The Emperor Arrives

Whilst up to this point the battle had been a complete success there was a certain deliberation as to what should take place next. Beyond the woods, scattered among a range of hills, was the entire Russian army. Whilst the discussion was taking place a rumour began to circulate. Fears soon gave way to enthusiasm when we spied the emperor, surrounded by his glittering staff, moving forward. Everybody hoped that his arrival meant that he was going to crown the brilliant day with glory.

Plate 30

The Evening of 26 July 1812

Between Ostrovno and Vitepsk

The King of Naples and the Prince galloped over to the Emperor to inform him of developments and to let him know what measures they had taken. Napoleon, in order to see for himself, went to the front lines and placed himself upon an eminence from where he was able to observe the enemy's dispositions and the nature of the terrain. In addition, he studied the enemy camp.

He conceived a plan and quickly set troops in motion or adjusted the dispositions of his own army. His orders were given calmly and transmitted with efficiency. Our soldiers moved through the woods and debouched onto the Vitepsk hills just as the sun was beginning to set.

Plate 31

The Evening of 26 July 1812

Between Ostrovno and Vitepsk

It was around eleven in the evening when Napoleon, after having ridden up and down the line, called off the attack. He urged the troops to prepare for the decisive encounter on the morrow. He placed himself among our skirmishers, and indeed dined with them, so he could observe the enemy. An enemy bullet wounded a man right next to him. The following hours were spent in reconnoitring the terrain and awaiting the arrival of reinforcements.

Plate 32

Noon, 27 July 1812

Before Vitepsk

The Viceroy's corps and Murat's cavalry advanced whilst three divisions of I Corps, under the orders of Lobau, attacked along the main road and pushed in the enemy's left. Fighting was fierce but of short duration. The Russian rearguard fell back behind the Luczissa ravine and formed up with the bulk of the Russian army, some 80,000 men.

Plate 33

27 July 1812

Before Vitepsk

Napoleon called a halt to hostilities around noon and the Viceroy established his camp in amongst his Guards. We were right in the centre of the battlefield, attempting to rest. The Viceroy's aides, as zealous as ever, sought to create a shelter for their Prince out of some interwoven branches in order to keep him out of the burning sun. The heat was so intense that even the strongest of men was reduced to inaction.

Plate 34

27 July 1812

On the Heights above Vitepsk

Vitepsk was romantically situated, surrounded as it is by rolling hills covered with lush vegetation and picturesque woods. Such a sight made an agreeable impression even on those who were familiar with the beauties of Italy. As the sun went down we caught sight of a majestic and rare spectacle. The sun's rays, which had shone on us all day, seemed to melt into a sea of fire for as far as the eye could see. The entire horizon was lit up and the sky's red hue was reflected all across the land. Flames from some burning villages and from part of Vitepsk itself soon began to make their presence felt, with columns of smoke advancing into the blood-red sky. It was an imposing tableau at once enchanting and grotesque. Not a soul was left untouched by this magnificent and profound sight.

Plate 35

28 July 1812

The Emperor at Vitepsk

We had marched for 18 miles through sand, pushing our way through blinding clouds of dust and oppressive heat, to reach Agaponovtchina at nightfall. Whilst the army collapsed from exhaustion and sought to quench its thirst, Napoleon, the King of Naples, the Viceroy and the Prince of Neuchatel held a council of war around the imperial tents which had been set up by an old castle alongside the main road.

Plate 36

14 August 1812

On the Road to Lianvavitschi

The different corps which composed the army were now seeking to concentrate around Razasna. Some were coming from Orsha, others from Babinovitschi, Liozna or Roudina. The Emperor arrived at Razasna on the morning of 13 August and had two divisions belonging to Davout's I Corps drawn up at Dubrovna. After having inspected the troops he had them join Davout's three other divisions and set the whole corps in motion along the road to Smolensk. Meanwhile V Corps, which formed our right, was also directed against this city, passing through Romanovo. This concentration of so many men in an area which resembled a desert augmented our plight and doubled the confusion which reigned along the main roads. Isolated soldiers sought in vain to catch up with their regiments whilst officers, carrying important orders, could not get through the congestion on the roads or around bridges or the terrible tumult one met with in any defile.

Plate 37

16 August 1812

The Artist

After many days of difficult marching we had a much-needed day of rest around Sinaki. For me it was one of the most enjoyable camps and I even found time to construct a little shelter which, for all its simplicity, seemed to me to be a palace. The weather was superb and I profited from it to put in order the many sketches I had made in the previous weeks. The camp situated amongst some stunning scenery, inspired me to produce this image.

It is not without emotion that I look upon the picture of my two excellent horses who endured so much by taking me to Moscow and from there all the way back to Minsk. That place would be the end of their journey for when we arrived in that pitiful town I was obliged to sell them both, and two others besides, for some four louis.

Plate 38

17 August 1812

The Viceroy's Camp

It was late into the night when we arrived in the spot seen here and where we might snatch a few hours' rest. Quite by chance we came across the wreckage of a cart and, after we had dragged it closer to the fire, this served as a comfortable bed for the Viceroy. Exhausted by our exertions, and weary with sleep, each sought to find a place around the fire and get some rest. Each rolled himself up in his greatcoat to keep out the disagreeable frost which was all the more uncomfortable as it contrasted so markedly with the heat endured during the day. It was at dawn on a sombre, cloudy day that I sketched this scene. No sooner had the first rays of light crept over the horizon than the Prince was again on the march heading for Smolensk.

The continual heat and the exhausting forced marches had considerably weakened the troops. It was also noticeable that the number of marauders, composed of men who had quitted the ranks, was on the increase. They swept the region on the lookout for food.

Plate 39

18 August 1812

Before Smolensk

The day after a battle is always woeful. Calculating casualties is a sorrowful task and one which played tricks. For, in order to make the right impression on our soldiers, we were in the habit of clearing the field of our dead as quickly as possible but leaving the enemy's fallen on display. Of course, it was also natural that we scoured the field for our own wounded, and tended to them, before turning our attention to those of our adversary. Here we see a group of French wounded; these are but a few selected from among the many victims of that bloody day at Smolensk.

Plate 40

18 August 1812

Smolensk

This image captures the scene as we enter the ruins of what was once a beautiful and handsome city. The Emperor's expression altered significantly when his eyes alighted on the smoking wastes where mounds of smouldering ash lay intermingled with hideous corpses, shrivelled in the fire. Such destruction astonished him. And what a victory for our troops. Instead of finding shelter, food and booty there was nothing but rubble on which to pitch our tents.

Plate 41

19 August 1812

Camp near Smolensk

The army had hoped in vain that victory at Smolensk would alleviate some of the woes it had been subjected to. The beautiful ancient city was a pile of ash and we were reduced to camping outside the smoking walls and contenting ourselves with our meagre rations. The heat of the day gave way to freezing nights and this, which seemed like a conspiracy to destroy our army, much affected the troops. Means were lacking to restore some of the soldiers' energy, by feeding them and resting them, and it has to be said that disgust and discouragement everywhere revealed themselves. Mental anguish and physical suffering weighed heavily on every individual.

The camps around Smolensk furnished me with sufficient examples of such a decline in the state of the army. Here is one such scene which I have attempted to capture accurately.

Plate 42

19 August 1812

Smolensk, seen from the North

Meanwhile the Russians maintained a stubborn hold on the northern suburb, on the right bank of the Dnepr. We spent much of the day and night of 18 August repairing bridges. Just before dawn on 19 August Marshal Ney crossed the river in the light of burning houses. At first he did battle with the flames and then he began to climb the slope on which the suburb was built. Our troops advanced slowly, cautiously, all the while attempting to keep clear of the flames. The Russians fought back, cleverly presenting themselves and barring further progress.

Ney and his troops advanced through a labyrinth of burning houses, eyes wide open, ever alert, but completely unaware that the Russians were not waiting for them at the top of the slope. They were not going to drive our men back down the incline and into the river. They had departed. But our troops halted, the Marshal being uncertain as to which road the Russians had taken – the one to St Petersburg or the one to Moscow. Seeing only cossacks before him, and having neither prisoners nor inhabitants to interrogate, Ney ordered his troops to halt at around noon.

Plate 43

20 August 1812

Before Smolensk

I sketched this image at dawn on 20 August. Columns of smoke rise from the suburb which has been consumed by the conflagration. In the foreground a group of Italian Guards are attempting to warm themselves after having emerged from their basic shelters. The climate in Russia was a real test for these soldiers, unaccustomed to such cold in the summer. For it was August and the days were hot and the nights were freezing. A cause for concern for all our soldiers.

Plate 44

25 August 1812

Prince Eugene near the Vopp

On the morning of the 25th we crossed the Vopp. It was a river which seemingly did not merit any attention but little did we know how fatal to our troops it would prove to be.

Still, we might have guessed that it would pose problems in winter as it proved to be relatively difficult to ford even in summer. The river was deep and the riverbanks so steep that the artillery could only cross after considerable exertions and by doubling the teams on the guns.

Plate 45

25 August 1812

Episode during the Crossing of the Vopp

The difficulties our troops, particularly our artillery, encountered in attempting to cross the Vopp meant that I was presented with an abundance of scenes in which stamina and perseverance came to the fore. In this simple sketch I have sought to provide for the viewer a true idea of what took place on that day.

Plate 46

26 August 1812

Crossing the Dnepr near Dorogobui

On the morning of the 26th, enjoying splendid weather, we arrived on the banks of the Dnepr. The Viceroy, constant in the care he bestowed upon the movement of his troops, often supervising in person the minutest of details, paused here whilst attempts to repair a bridge the Russians had destroyed were made. His presence raised the spirits of the men working on the bridge and the passage across the river was soon available. As the water was not very deep a body of infantry waded across the river but when some cavalry and artillery attempted to do the same they encountered all manner of difficulties including some strong currents.

Plate 47

28 August 1812

On the Road to Viazma

The heroic and noble character of Prince Eugene is known to posterity but his humane nature and the attention he showed upon mankind caused him to be respected by friend and foe alike. I was fortunate enough to be a witness to many of his acts of generosity which, despite his many military preoccupations, shone forth and helped keep at bay the maladies of want and affliction. I will now give an example.

One summer's day, in oppressive heat, we had been marching along next to a column of Bavarian cavalry. We passed through the dark savage pine forests that surrounded Viazma. The dust kicked up by the marching troops was suffocating and the sandy road burning hot. Everyone suffered. Quite by chance the Prince passed closed by a woman. She was mounted on a thin horse, which seemed crushed by a pile of luggage, and was attempting to feed an infant balancing it with difficulty on her knees. The sight perhaps affected the Prince's paternal instincts as he was so far from home, and he spent much time lavishing attention on a child which had started life in such trying circumstances. Calling over one of his aides-de-camp, Monsieur de Saive, who spoke German fluently, he sought details of the child and the condition of the mother. He learnt that the baby had been born on the road, that he was just five weeks old and that he was doing well. He presented some gold coins to the woman, bade her farewell in an affable manner and modesty obliged him to turn a deaf ear to the praise which his action had given rise to.

Plate 48

28 August 1812

At Viazma

The town was built around the source of the river which bore the same name and, although surrounded by splendid gullies and valleys, sat on a plateau which dominated the surrounding countryside and the defile through which the Smolensk road passed.

We had only just arrived when the town fell victim to a fire. Although we were by now used to seeing such sights, we could not help but be overwhelmed by a sense of pity on this unfortunate city of 10,000 souls. Founded relatively recently it had more than 30 churches and its larger houses had been built with elegance and taste. Now all was shrouded in smoke. The city's destruction was all the more regrettable since we had seen nothing as attractive as this place since quitting Vitepsk. Two battalions of the 25th Line were sent into Viazma to fight the flames and they managed to save two-thirds of the deserted city. The entire population had fled towards Moscow adding to the vast numbers of refugees reportedly making for the capital.

Plate 49

30 August 1812

Near Viazma

The area around Viazma was very attractive, rolling hills bordered fertile fields, and rich meadows stretched on as far as Borodino. But there it seemed that nature itself had prepared to go on the defensive and was ready for the terrible combat that would be fought around the village. There a plain, covered in sandy-red dust, stretched forwards, our vision broken by a few clumps of trees. It was nothing but a vast field of battle.

But, favoured by good weather, the army, although hungry, managed to snatch some days' rest after all the hard marching. This would be the lull before the storm as soon we would be at the throat of the Russian army, pitched into a confrontation which seemed to assure mutual destruction.

Plate 50

5th September 1812, the Morning

By the Moskva

On the morning of the 5th, IV Corps, on the left flank of the army, advanced rapidly. Pushing through a forest we were troubled by cossacks but drove them back through some partially-destroyed villages. The desolation caused by these horsemen meant that it was relatively easy to follow their traces. As we approached a hill we spied several of their squadrons drawn up in battle formation beneath the walls of an attractive country house.

The Viceroy had the Bavarians advance against these troops and the Germans, despite the difficulties presented by the terrain, arrived at the summit in good order. The enemy retreated down the reverse slope, pursued by some roundshot fired by our guns now placed in the grounds of the country house. Following the cossacks we soon came across Russian columns making their way towards a huge plateau. It was here, it seemed, that Prince Kutuzov was drawing up his army for a trial of strength. On our right we could see the Kolotskoi abbey, its multitude of towers making it seem like a miniature city. The domes on these towers were glittering in the sunshine and shone through the clouds of dust raised by our numerous cavalry. It was a sight to contrast the sombre, even savage, nature of the surrounding countryside. The plain before the Russian position was devoid of supplies, the fields had been harvested, the villages burnt to the ground and so it was that we had nothing to eat, nothing to feed our horses and nothing in which to take shelter.

Plate 51

5 September 1812, the Evening

By Borodino

Later that day Prince Eugene ordered Delzons' and Broussier's divisions to advance. The Italian Guard, left in the rear, was placed in reserve. The two divisions had scarcely arrived on a small height opposite the enemy redoubt when heavy fighting broke out to our right. Here skirmishers belonging to Gerard's division (part of I Corps) were engaging the enemy. Our troops initially managed to advance to a ravine separating the two sides but were then pushed back.

Further to the right was a Russian redoubt between two woods close to the village of Shevarino and fire from that position caused consternation in our ranks. They had built this position to strengthen their left, the weakest part of their line. Napoleon saw at once that it would be necessary to take this position and bestowed the honour of doing so on Compans' division (I Corps). These brave troops formed up in attack columns and advanced against the Russians with sufficient ardour to successfully conclude their enterprise. Meanwhile, Prince Poniatowski advanced some cavalry to turn the Russian position. Compans' troops were soon engaged and, after nearly an hour, managed to seize the Russian position. The enemy sought to counter-attack but was completely beaten. Finally, around ten in the evening, they abandoned the woods and fled in disorder towards the centre of their main body.

Compans' division proved itself worthy on that occasion but could only do so by sustaining heavy casualties.

A thousand of our troops paid in blood for this position. On the following morning Napoleon was reviewing the 61st Line, which had suffered heavily in the attack. When the Emperor asked where one of his battalions was, the colonel replied: 'Sire, it is in the redoubt.'

Plate 52

5 September 1812, the Evening

By the Moskva River

That evening the fighting died away as sunset put an end to the combat. The Viceroy, calm and collected as ever, returned to camp pursued by some Russian shells sent over from their position. One of the shells fell close to where we were and the Prince turned to those close to him and jested: 'Sirs, those of you with good horses better make use of them as this one could do us ill.' Indeed, the shell exploded shortly after but without harming anyone.

Plate 53

6 September 1812

Near Borodino

Nothing was quieter than the day which went before the battle of Borodino. It was almost prearranged. Why cause trouble today when tomorrow will decide the outcome once and for all? Even so, there was much to prepare. Each corps looked to their weapons, their units, their ammunition; stragglers were brought in to fill out the ranks which had been thinned by the constant advance. The generals looked over their dispositions for the attack, or how they might go on the defensive, and studied the terrain with care to leave nothing to chance.

 The two colossal armies eyed each other suspiciously, preparing in silence for the unavoidable shock of collision.

Plate 54

6 September 1812

View of the Battlefield

Daylight had presented to us the imposing spectacle of the entire Russian army drawn up along some heights which curved around to form some kind of amphitheatre. We examined their position and saw much activity as they prepared for this important battle which might decide the fate of Russia.

A mournful silence continued to reign on both sides, rendering the sight of both armies somewhat morbid. The silence was only broken by the discharge from a Russian battery along with some skirmishing along the ravines which separated the two sides.

I made good use of this day to outline the exact contours of the field upon which the memorable battle would be fought. In this plate and the next I have tried to present the Russian position as it was, space permitting, and my plan conforms more or less to what Labaume has also recorded.

Plate 55

6 September 1812

View of the Battlefield

Here is Labaume's account by way of comparison:

'I went forwards and saw that the Russians had drawn themselves up behind the Kolotscha on a series of plateaux. Their left seemed much weakened by the loss of the redoubt we had seized the evening before. We also seemed to dominate the village of Borodino which was an extremely important point protected by a small stream which ran into the Kolotscha. On the plateau three redoubts had been built and the largest of them was also the strongest. It had fired on us the previous evening. The other two were based around the ruins of a hamlet which had been broken up to allow artillery to be positioned there. The earthworks had been hastily constructed and the ditches before them insignificant.

On our extreme left the Italian cavalry had crossed the stream but Borodino, guarded by a strong body of enemy troops, remained in Russian hands. The terrain was almost completely in range of their principal batteries and other guns positioned along the banks of the stream. On our right, it was clear that our success the evening before had meant that we could push right up against Kutuzov's left flank and approach the main redoubt across the plain.'

Plate 56

7 September 1812

Battle of Borodino

The Russians were initially shocked by the onslaught but, animated by Kutuzov and Yermolov, they recovered. Our 30th Line, alone against an entire army, dared charge forward with the bayonet. It was surrounded, crushed and chased from the redoubt leaving behind a good third of its soldiers along with its intrepid commander, pierced by more than 20 bayonets. The Russians, encouraged, no longer contented themselves with acting defensively. They began to attack.

So it was that all that the art of war could offer, and all the fire and fury of man, was present here at this one spot. The French army maintained itself beneath this volcano for more than four hours, showered with shot and shell. It took all of Prince Eugene's tenacity, and the experience of men who had vanquished upon many such an occasion to hold on and not admit defeat.

Nearly every division lost its general. The Viceroy went from one to another, mixing praise with reproach in equal measure, and encouraging the men by recalling past victories. He informed the Emperor of the critical position he had been placed in but Napoleon replied that 'he could do nothing; that it was up to him to triumph and that he had to make just one final effort to win the day'.

Plate 57

7 September 1812

The Taking of the Great Redoubt

So it was that the Russians reformed their left wing for the third time to bar Ney and Murat's progress. The latter called upon Montbrun's cavalry to advance but that general was killed. Caulaincourt came up to replace him but found the general's aides-de-camp mourning his loss. Turning to them he cried, 'Follow me! Do not mourn him, revenge him!' Murat showed the cavalry the Russian position. They had to climb the heights by the Russian batteries and, whilst the light cavalry exploited the breakthrough, the heavies were to swing round and take the Russian redoubt in the rear whilst Eugene's men attacked frontally. Caulaincourt replied, 'You'll see me there within the hour, dead or alive.' He advanced, crushing all before him, then swung left with his cuirassiers and burst into the bloody redoubt. But there he was hit by a bullet and knocked from his horse. His victory was his tomb.

Plate 58

7 September 1812

On the Field of Battle

Among the many victims of this day we had great cause to regret the loss of Count Wittgenstein, colonel of a Bavarian light cavalry regiment. He was hit by a roundshot fired from a redoubt and mortally wounded. He died a hero a few hours later. Of his regiment, just 30 men and two officers remained that evening. The rest had been wounded or killed.

As Ségur said, the losses of the day were immense and the achievements were not in proportion. Everyone around the Emperor had somebody to mourn, be it a friend, relative or brother. Losses were heavy among the officers and some 43 generals were killed or wounded. What woe in Paris! What a triumph for our enemies!

Plate 59

7 September 1812

Italian Guards of Honour

This picture of a group of men from this unit, warming themselves around a fire made from the wood from destroyed wagons, presents an insight into how our men, who had suffered so many privations in the course of this campaign, were deprived of any means of subsistence even after the battle.

A sense of the sadness caused by the vast distance these men were from their glorious country, the memory of fallen brothers in arms and, finally, bleak presentiments of what the future might hold, lend these warriors profoundly reflective expressions.

That night was cold and damp although the weather during the day had been magnificent. The army camped on the battlefield, partly in the redoubts which had been so gloriously captured. Our situation was cruel, neither man nor horse had anything to eat and the lack of firewood meant that we felt all the rigours of this cold, wet night.

Plate 60

8 September 1812

On the Field of Battle

Everything conspired to render the battlefield one of the most ghastly there ever was. The sky was overcast, there were icy showers and strong gusts of wind. Houses were ruined, the plain was covered with debris. The horizon was dotted with clumps of sombre northern trees. Everywhere soldiers wandered among the corpses, seeking food in the backpacks of fallen comrades. Wounds were horrible, as Russian bullets were bigger than our own. In camp all was quiet. No more singing, no more talking. Mournful silence held sway.

Officers and NCOs, commanding handfuls of soldiers, remained around the colours. Clothes were battle-torn and stained with powder and drenched in blood. Even so, among all this misery, in the midst of this disaster, there was a sense of pride. When the Emperor came into view there were some cries of triumph, although such were rare. In such an army, capable at once of enthusiasm and analysis, each individual weighed the future of the whole.

The battle, which was to decide the fate of Europe, was fought with a determination that bordered on despair. For that reason the only prisoners taken were those who had been wounded. In this scene we present a few wounded Russian prisoners guarded by French dragoons.

However, the most shocking sight was the vast quantity of dead which covered the battlefield, making it a place which froze one's blood with horror.

Plate 61

8 September 1812

On the Field of Battle

The day after the battle nature itself seemed to be in mourning. The sombre sky was full of clouds, a cold north-westerly wind was blowing across the arid plain on which the battle had been fought. The scene was one which filled me with horror. I felt paralysed and, only by calling to mind the countless other horrors I had been witness to in this frightful campaign, could I shake myself from my stupor. Having done so I made myself capture a few aspects of the scene on paper. In this sketch you can see the heights upon which the Great Redoubt was constructed with the village of Borodino in the background. The battlefield is strewn with dead and wounded. There were parts of the field where an exploding shell had knocked down whole ranks of men and horses. Such losses meant that piles of corpses were heaped across the plain and the space in between was filled with discarded weapons, lances, helmets and cuirasses.

Plate 62

8 September 1812

On the Moscow Road

After capturing the village of Borodino some of Prince Eugene's men crossed the Kologha and made it to the main road which would take the French army to the gates of Moscow. The horrible passage of that river made it worthy to be remembered in this scene, another reminder of this dreadful campaign.

Three weeks after the battle, after I was recrossing the field after departing from Moscow, I found a group of Russian wounded gathered on the banks of the river by the little bridge. They had slept in the open and had prolonged their miserable existence by eating flesh from dead horses. A few were still able to speak but most were dying or in their final agonies. Not far away a young foal sought milk from its dead mother.

How could such scenes not fill one with despair.

Plate 63

9 September 1812

Between Mojaisk and Moscow

The Russians had withdrawn from Borodino without leaving any traces behind them. That had been the case at Vitepsk and Smolensk too but this time it was all the more remarkable given the scale of the battle which had just been fought. We remained uncertain between the Moscow and Kaluga roads until Mortier and Murat pressed on towards Moscow. Without supplies, our men ate horsemeat or pillaged grain as they advanced finding no sign of the Russian army. Although the infantry of the latter formed a confused mass, they left no debris in their wake. Perhaps it was patriotism or the habit of discipline which held together their army, thus depriving us of all manner of information. Also lacking were supplies as we marched across this barren landscape.

Plate 64

10 September 1812

Zvenigorod Abbey

This abbey dominated the River Moskva. With its twenty-foot high and six-foot thick crenellated walls and four towers on each corner of the battlements it seemed a fortress. Built in the thirteenth or fourteenth century this building called to mind the ancient Muscovites, full of admiration for their priests, making religious authority surpass that of noble power. Or of the Czar with the patriarch of Moscow leading his horse by the bridle in some ceremony. But the monks, so powerful in the days before Peter the Great, were reduced to a simpler life when this monarch established his power and confiscated their wealth.

Plate 65

10 September 1812

Imperial Guard Grenadiers near Mojaisk

After Borodino our army advanced on Moscow in three columns. Napoleon, impatient to seize the capital of the Russian empire and with his usual impetuosity, pursued the enemy along the road from Smolensk whilst Prince Poniatowski, at the head of V Corps, swept along the Kaluga road. The Viceroy, with IV Corps, formed the left flank and moved along the Zvenigorod road heading for Moscow, before which, it was supposed, the army would concentrate.

Plate 66

10 September 1812

Marauders near Moscow

This scene represents some of those marauders who, at this time, represented such a substantial part of the army. They combed the Russian countryside in their thousands, seizing all they could find in order to prolong their sordid existence.

The two mounted soldiers belong to the artillery train. One wears a woman's fur coat dyed a fetching pink colour. Such a costume contrasts remarkably with the worn faces of French veterans. Their wagon has been seized from some Russians.

Plate 67

20 September 1812

The French Army before Moscow

Here was the army camped a few miles before Moscow, so hopeful that the trials and tribulations were now at an end and that respite awaited them in the capital. This camp was perhaps the last one the French army would enjoy and it is characterised by its military bearing. Despite being exhausted, weakened by forced marches and reduced to half of its effectives by combat, it was still a great army commanded by a great captain and one which had braved all the obstacles the Russian terrain and climate could present. But once it reached Moscow its fate was sealed. Looking at this scene, which of us cannot prevent the sad reflection from escaping his lips that 'those legions of heroes no longer exist'.

Plate 68

20 September 1812

Moscow

On this day large parts of Moscow were nothing more than smouldering ruins. The dye was cast, fortune was reversed and here it was that providence put an end to the glories hitherto enjoyed by the French army.

The soldiers were depressed having to deal with nothing but woe and were prey to dark presentiments. Having been exhausted by forced marches, afflicted by all manner of privation and particularly by the lack of food, and deprived of clothing which might resist the rigours of bad weather, very few of them were in any condition to even consider what lay in store for them. Soon they would succumb, unfortunates, to the terrible storm which would be unleashed upon them.

On 20 and 21 September elements of the army began to move into the city from Peterskoi where Napoleon had stayed whilst the fire ravaged the city. A few sentries were posted here and there among the smoking cinders, all that remained of this fine imperial city, whilst bands of unfortunate men sought shelter in vain. Others, motivated by abject want, searched high and low for food but there were also others, inspired by greed, who sought to acquire booty even though it could little benefit them in such desperate circumstances. Everyone was in a state of confused desperation and none really knew what they were looking for.

Plate 69

20 September 1812

Moscow

The effect the destruction of Moscow had on individual soldiers was, of course, diverse, and it offered an attentive observer a rich variety of subjects to study. On the whole, the vast majority were overcome by discouragement, partly induced by the long ordeal they had been through and by the fact that they had seen all their hopes for a better future, and for an end to their sufferings, go up in smoke.

Some of the more reflective soldiers were absorbed by sombre contemplation of what might now come to pass. Those of a more insensitive nature allowed themselves the liberty to do as they pleased and to profit from the opportunity. Discipline, so vital for the working of such a vast host, was gone and violence and selfishness overcame order. True, a mass of provisions had been found in Moscow but the disorder which reigned in the city put paid to any attempt to distribute such supplies fairly. Everyone, by guile or by force, sought to get his hands on anything which might prove useful.

So it was that one day, whilst passing through the ruins, I came across a body of drunken cavalrymen dragging along with them whatever they could carry and shouting at each other to hurry up. One of them was riding a horse carrying a basket loaded with bottles and supplies. He was so completely drunk that he tottered this way and that until his horse made a sharp movement, sending the man sprawling on the floor along with his booty. His comrades laughed heartily, drunk as they were, at the scene.

Plate 70

22 September 1812

Moscow

The violence of the fire which engulfed Moscow was matched by the ferocity of the French soldiers as they watched the destruction. But the army of camp-followers, servants, sutlers and so on which follows in the wake of any army, committed its fair share towards the sacking of the city. Horses, vehicles, furniture, tools, paintings, works of art, and all manner of other objects which were of no immediate need to anyone, all were seized and dragged into courtyards or onto street-corners and sold off. Most of the looters were drunk and this meant that they frequently fell to quarrelling over their booty, resulting in bloody and battered faces.

It had been an army previously distinguished by its fine martial bearing and its appearance, its love of order, sentiments of heroism and honour. Now, it was revolting to behold and it was a sight which convinced me that I should now return to my homeland and no longer play the witness to inevitable ruin. Firm in my resolve, I prepared to set off, deaf to those who warned me of the dangers of such a journey, not so that I might avoid the deplorable fate of the army but that I might escape the effects such disgusting scenes were having upon me.

Plate 71

22 September 1812

Moscow

Here is the man who shaped the events which so characterised an age so unforgettable to those who lived through it. A hero who, at the head of a valiant army, threatened to overthrow the governments of Europe and overturn the continent's thrones. But a hero who, in the ash of Moscow, met the end of his glorious career. And at what cost was the effort to end the gigantic march of this man made? Only an enormous sacrifice for Russia won victory.

No image can truly capture the terrible scene of burning Moscow, only those who saw the city prey to flames can recall the horror which so gripped the soul. Here I have placed a portrait of the hero of the age before the smouldering ruins of Moscow as they menace him with cries of 'Here your career shall end!'

Plate 72

Epilogue

With the gracious permission of my sovereign, I left Moscow on 24 September 1812 after the flames had died down. I equipped myself with sufficient money for the journey and enough food for 15 days. I was accompanied by a servant who could speak Russian and a 60-year-old veterinary surgeon in the service of the King of Bavaria who had come to Moscow with a transport of horses and who now wished to return home.

Shortly after leaving Moscow we came across the field of Borodino. I stopped my carriage for a time and took a walk over what seemed to me to be an interesting part of the battlefield, but I saw so much that was hideous and shocking, and found the air so polluted, that I soon turned back.

Most of the corpses of men and horses had been left unburied and it was a horrific sight, if I were to give you a true account of the field 18 days after the battle. The most touching scene was that of seven men, who had crawled together next to a dead horse. Five of them were out of their misery; death had ended their martyrdom; but two were still alive and could speak and move a little. I couldn't take them with me, nor could I get them help. I confess, that for a moment, I had the idea that I should put them out of their misery.

Horror-struck, I ran from this scene of hell. Breathing heavily, I said to myself: 'Yes, war is the most terrible thing!' Those unfortunates were Russians, who had lain helplessly on the ground for eighteen days in such a state.

Whenever I told this tale, I was asked what had kept those men alive for so long. I cannot answer this question, as I did not speak their language and they were not in any condition to talk much, but I think that they must have been eating the horse by which they lay.

The battlefield of Borodino is of very gloomy aspect, but now it appeared to be a hideous desert. I encountered nobody for hours; it seemed that no one wanted to be here; they all passed by as quickly as possible.

The impression that everything made on us was heightened by the melancholy weather. My veterinary was pleased when I returned; he had no wish to walk around the battlefield and was sitting impatiently in the carriage.

I was deeply depressed and we went silently on our way along the devastated road, which everywhere showed the traces of the fighting. Later we came upon an abbey, which gave us hope that we might find quarters there, but we found it was a field hospital, which gave us another horror show and urged us on our way.

Towards evening a large barn offered passable quarters for us and the horses for the night. We made tea, without sugar or milk, as we had neither, and we ate the rest of the mutton. But the terrible things that I had seen that day kept filling my dreams with awful fantasies.

Next day brought us a terrible storm; we trudged on amid wind, rain and snow showers through the 29th on the muddy road. It was the sixth day of our continuous journey. Due to the poor diet and the bad road, our horses began to show fatigue. The prevailing westerly wind caused us great discomfort. Strange to say, the days were very stormy, but the nights were mostly calm and fine.

That afternoon we met some travelling companions, Jewish salesmen from Glogau. Businesslike as they were, they had followed the army to Moscow to find trade and seemed to be returning in quite a happy state. They looked well and in good spirits, three fairly young men-of-the-world who knew how to conduct themselves. From their dress and appearance, they did not seem, at first sight, to be Jewish. They had studied and were well on the way to becoming part of the intelligentsia.

Their transport consisted of a canvas-covered wagon pulled by four good horses. They seemed very keen to attach themselves to me; I was not overjoyed at the prospect, for, as a matter of principle, I like to travel alone; but I could not stop them.

The hope that we might find reasonable quarters in Viazma was soon dashed; it was so bad that we could scarcely wait until morning to leave this town behind us; a place in which we had been a month before, in fine autumnal weather, full of high hopes of success.

We moved off in finer weather and got to know our new travelling companions better. They seemed to appreciate travelling with an officer from the retinue of the Viceroy and paid me a measure of respect.

I also wanted to convince myself – in the modesty with which I undertook everything – that they would help bring some more courage and hope into our journey. They also had some coffee and sugar and offered to sell some to us quite cheaply.

At midday we made a lucky find of forage in a village; that was a great gift; we fed the poor horses, which ate with gusto, and took a goodly supply with us. Towards evening we spotted a small village on a hill and made for it. At least the horses were out of the wind and rain and had a good supper.

Here we found several poor French soldiers, sick and helpless, who had sought shelter in the huts. Two of these dragged themselves up to our fire like ghosts and asked to be allowed to warm themselves a little. They looked awful and I felt very sorry for them; I gave them some hot soup, which they took with shaking hands and gulped down greedily. Then they curled up under my wagon and seemed to go to sleep; I didn't want to disturb them and let them lie. Next morning one of them was dead and the other almost so.

Next day, 1 October, there were more rumours that cossacks were raiding the road. That scared the pants off my Israelite travelling companions; they at once began to drive very fast, which I was loath to do on account of my horses and my much heavier carriage. Then I had a stroke of luck. I met a group of French soldiers, who had three horses on their wagon. After a lot of haggling, I managed to buy, for a reasonable price, a fine horse that was at once put into harness.

Now we had four horses and made better speed; towards evening we reached the town of Semlevo. Here things looked really bad. The entrances were blocked with palisades and all sorts of obstructions and we had difficulty getting them to let us in. The small garrison was scared of being raided and they were surprised to hear that we had come from Moscow. We found some miserable lodgings; we were almost always in such a state in the towns. At least in the country we had fresh air; in the towns the atmosphere was poisonous. As soon as we reached Semlevo, I went to garrison headquarters and found some helpful officers there. They were most interested to hear from me all about the conditions in Moscow and of our experiences on the way back.

'I am really very surprised', said the commandant, 'that you got here so easily, but I have to tell you, that you won't get to Smolensk; we hear that the cossacks are stopping everything from four miles out from the city, and they're frequently on our backs here. We have to send out large military patrols to find food and forage, for we have nothing here and our situation is miserable.'

'That's bad news', I answered, 'but what do you want with me here? You say yourself, that you are short of everything, why do you want to add two more guests to your problems? I do not doubt the truth of that which you have been kind enough to tell me, but since I left Moscow I have heard the same story, and you have to admit, that the same dangers which lie before me, are behind me as well. No one knows what Napoleon will decide to do and I cannot convince myself that I should stay here in indecision. I am determined to continue my journey to Smolensk.'

There were three French officers here, who had been lightly wounded at Borodino. They were now well enough to travel. They had been hanging around in Semlevo for days already. They listened to our conversation keenly; agreed with me and decided to join me on the journey.

We left Semlevo early in a cold mist and soon met a chasseur à cheval, who was a sentry on the road. He looked gloomy and frozen and shouted to us in a deep bass voice: 'You'll meet cossacks within a quarter of an hour!' But he made no effort to stop us. My new companions were visibly shaken. They said that to continue in such mist was dangerous; we should at least wait until it had cleared, as we might bump into the cossacks before we became aware of them.

I answered that we should not let ourselves be so easily scared. The mist also hid us from the cossacks; they wouldn't be directly on the road, at least that was how I interpreted their operational tactics. Anyway, I had not the slightest intention of talking them into coming along with me; I was not responsible for them and was acting in my own interests; they might as well do as they pleased, I was going on.

That was what I did, and the officers trailed along, some way behind us, moving as slowly as snails.

We had not gone far, when our situation seemed really to be getting serious. An officer on foot hurried out of a side road to meet us; I slowed down a little. He caught up with us and asked us in French to stop. He was a tall, well-built man, of commanding speech and appearance. After the usual questions; 'Where have you come from? Where are you bound?' he began to tell us that he was 'the colonel of a Polish infantry regiment, that is on the march here. Yesterday evening, I left the main road to spend the night in a chateau that I know. I found lodgings there and had no worries about staying there, as I had a strong military escort with me. But during the night I was woken by gunshots; the cossacks had attacked in force; my men were captured after a brave fight, and I lost my horse and all my belongings. I escaped in the dark and, as you see, I have nothing else apart from my sword. You will meet my regiment; the cossacks will let it pass – they always avoid combat with large bodies of infantry. It is a fine regiment and would fight to the last. Tell the officers what has happened to me and tell them to speed up their march; I will await them in Semlevo.

'If you have the courage to continue on your way, I wish you better luck than I had!'

So we parted. This tale certainly caused us to reconsider our plan; we could expect nothing good today.

After about an hour, we met the regiment, which to our surprise, was still in good order and very numerous. They took up the whole road, and there were strong patrols to each side. The officers were very disturbed to hear my story, and told me that the cossacks had not dared to attack them, but all train and wagons that they met were lost and fell into their hands. The escorts had defended themselves, some were killed, the rest wounded or captured. All the horses that had been following their regiment had also been taken. The cossacks had then taken post in a wood so that it was not possible for infantry to get near them.

This was now too much for the three officers from Semlevo

who had dared to come this far. One of them turned to me and said: 'Now, young man, what do you say to that?'

'It looks very dangerous, but I am not turning back', I replied.

'Allez', he said scornfully, 'You are a fool!'

They had a small Russian wagon with three horses with them. As they were now in the middle of the regiment, they could not turn around. They unhitched the horses, swung themselves up on them and rode for Semlevo for all they were worth.

Afterwards, I often thought about these three gentlemen, and whether they were as lucky as I was, to see their homeland again. I doubt it; they were not over-endowed with courage and resolution.

After the regiment had passed, we went slowly and carefully on our way, and in half an hour we came to the site of the cossack attack. Two dead lay in their own blood, and the smoking wreckage of ammunition wagons and other vehicles showed where the fighting had been shortly before. I cannot deny that this scene affected our courage, neither can I conceal our relief that the cossacks had vanished; we didn't see them all day long.

Happy that my guardian angel was watching over me, I set forth on my journey. I always seemed to come upon these battlegrounds after the crisis had passed. A couple of hours earlier or later and the situation might have been very different.

Without further trouble, we moved on and towards evening we came upon a sizeable inn, off to the side of the road. I would have passed on, but the noise of a mighty row caught my ear. I halted, listened, and established that a serious argument was taking place. Soon a well-known voice was heard. It was so loud, that you could have heard it from a quarter of an hour away. I clearly recognized that Swabian accent; I dismounted and went inside. Here I found the baggage of the Crown Prince of Württemberg. Some of the cavalry of the escort had fallen out and were fighting among themselves. At my appearance, the noise gradually abated. My Jews were there and added their voices to the row. They had been scared by the rumours

yesterday and had hurried on and met the Württembergers.

In the inn I made good friends with a royal stableman, who was with the escort. He was an educated man, with whom I later spent many hours. I travelled on with this escort, which included the servants, some fine riding horses, vehicles and mounted Jägers.

However pleasant I found the company – for the Jews had also joined in – I could not help thinking that it was always the larger convoys that were attacked by the cossacks, and I was safer if I went on alone and less likely to be noticed. On the tenth day of our journey the sky cleared, the air turned mild and we enjoyed one of the best autumn days in the whole of October. There followed days on which one could discard one's overcoat and not even think of one's fur. Unhindered, we went on and reached a small village by evening, where we found good lodgings. The next day was the same; we wandered along in a large group without any alarms. With such good weather, we didn't even try to find a village. We set up camp at the most appropriate spot and sat around the fire, in the best of spirits, eating, drinking and talking until midnight.

On the twelfth day of the journey I came across a problem: the horses' strength suddenly plunged and my driver became difficult. We had great difficulty in making progress and thereby lost our company, as we could not keep up. We spent the night in a wood. Next day we met the Württembergers again and spent a pleasant evening in a chateau in a convivial setting that regaled us with a splendid sight as the sun set.

At moments like this, one forgets one's past troubles and draws new strength.

On the fourteenth day we had to combat many problems. Our horses were so weak that they could scarcely walk. The harness kept breaking apart and to crown it all, we lost our way, lost our company and reached Smolensk with difficulty only at the evening. Here we had put the greatest dangers and the worst problems behind us, but great difficulties still lay ahead.

What effort it had taken us to travel 130 hours' distance in 14 days! What distances still lay between us and our beloved fatherland! Until we reached Smolensk, neither the weather nor anything else had affected my health; I reached that city strong and perfectly healthy; courage and decision had not left me for a minute.

During a two-day stay there, I had the harness repaired as well as could be and equipped myself with forage and some food (there was not much to be had). The men and the horses benefited from the rest. Smolensk was pretty full of French soldiers, but they seemed to be mostly stragglers and convalescents from the hospitals; there was no large garrison. I was thus not tempted to stay long.

On 10 October, with well-fed and rested horses, we set off again in beautiful weather and made good progress. I had taken the road to Minsk and aimed to go on via Grodno and Warsaw. That would have been the most direct route, but in Minsk I met new difficulties. The first two days' march from Smolensk to Minsk went very well. On the first night I found good lodgings in a pretty village, but on the second it was very bad. But you don't really bother about this sort of thing as long as you find some sort of shelter from wind and rain.

On 13 October we came upon two abbeys fairly close together. The first was for monks and looked very inviting from the outside, so we tried to find accommodation there. But right at the gate, a priest appeared and forbade us entry. His whole being radiated holiness, so we moved on. Shortly afterwards we came to a convent; here no one barred our entry into the walled courtyard; the gate was missing. The main building was shut, so we didn't bother to disturb the nuns, but took up quarters in one of the outbuildings in the yard. We could at once tell that we were not the first guests to have been here. It was wrecked and dirty and had neither doors nor windows.

Here we had a peculiar, almost comical adventure, but it did not seem so funny at first. As there were no stables, I had the horses let into one of the rooms in which there was not much to damage. Leading off this was a small cubby-hole with a place for a bed – but no bed. The vet and the driver settled in here, using our small remaining supply of hay as pillows. I settled down in the carriage, as the room was too dirty and the night was mild.

Suddenly I was woken by a great scream of fear and the stamping of the horses. I felt sure that my men were being beaten or killed. With my sabre in my hand I jumped down from the carriage. By the pale glow of a light in one of the convent windows, I saw my horse dragging my driver around the floor by his hair. He had smelled the hay under the driver's head and tried to get it. Now the hair was snagged in his teeth and he could not let go. This was due to the fact that the driver had long, curly hair, that was in a bit of a mess due to our present lifestyle. My vet tried to help, but as the horse kept walking backwards, pulling and pulling, and as the other horses were stamping around, he could not do the job alone. Even the two of us had great difficulties in freeing the driver.

Thus our night's sleep, in the solitude of the convent, which we had looked forward to so much, was rudely disturbed. The driver got off with a few kicks and a shock. A Polack like that can put up with a lot!

The next day, 14 October, was an ominous day; we lost our way early on, went far astray and upset the vehicle, but did no real damage, and at midday we reached a small village where we found food and forage in abundance. We thought that we could help ourselves, and the horses obviously enjoyed the hay. But we were soon taught otherwise.

A group of peasants appeared with the landowner at their head. They seemed very aggressive and wanted nothing better than to beat us up. The landlord came forward and asked me why we had left the main road? There were magazines there. This was not a military road and so on. There was nothing for it but to outwit him. I acted more aggressively than the peasants. I shouted at them that I had left the road because there were insufficient supplies in the magazine there, as I had a train of 60 horses that were coming up behind. I had come on ahead to scout out the way and to find quarters for the night. This story, and my confident manner, worked the trick.

They decided to negotiate. The landlord assured me that we could reach a large chateau easily before nightfall, where the lodgings would be much better than here. He painted a really rosy picture of it. Initially I played the sceptic and took out a four-page map of Russia from the wagon and spread it out on the ground. I poked about on it and played the situation out as long as possible, so that the horses could eat their fill. This ploy worked so well, that in the end they offered me money to go away. I rejected this indignantly; then wrote some lines of Italian on a piece of paper and gave it to him, saying that he could give this to a sergeant when my men arrived; they were Italians, who had great difficulty making themselves understood, but this would tell them to keep moving. Thus we were out of a fix and went off with our well-satisfied horses as fast as possible. A good hour before darkness we reached the chateau that we had been promised. The lord and his wife were of the educated class. I entered politely; explained that we were lost and requested to be able to enjoy their hospitality until next morning.

They welcomed me in and treated me as a not unwelcome guest. The food was very good. We set off again next morning and that evening we found a very pretty little village off to the side of the road. My driver told me that everything was not quite what it seemed here. All sorts of men were creeping around the carriage, and he had overheard some remarks, which made him prick up his ears, I ought to be watchful and have someone else sleep in the carriage as well. I told him that it was not so dangerous; they would scarcely murder me, and I could guard against robbery. As a precaution, I laid two loaded pistols on the seat beside me.

My driver was right; during the night I felt someone fiddling with the box and heard murmured voices. I did not move, but grabbed my pistols and cocked them both, which could be clearly heard outside. At that, all fell silent; then someone tried to enter the carriage, putting his hand through the leather blind. I gave it a heavy blow with the barrel of the pistol, whereupon he fell back; I then heard many footsteps running away. I was not disturbed again.

Next morning we met a poor Jew, who acted as our guide for some hours for a little money and led us back to the military road that I had to follow according to my marching orders.

The entire way from Moscow, I had learned that to leave the military road was to court danger. During the two days that we had been off that road, we had not met one soldier of the French army, and thus we could have been murdered without anyone bothering in the slightest. Now the statement of the landlord that magazines had been set up on the military road proved to be true. We drew forage and fed the poor horses; it was just such a shame that they had almost died on the journey here.

We went on wearily, but without event, for the next six days, until 22 October, when we were three hours from Minsk.

It had taken us four weeks of countless difficulties and dangers to cover a journey of 200 hours. You can easily imagine what damage such a trip does to one's clothing and equipment. The condition of the horses was really pitiful; it broke my heart just to look at them. They were in such a poor state that they could scarcely walk. On that last day, it took them a whole day to cover the distance that a pedestrian could cover in three hours.

When we left Moscow, a beautiful moonlit night had followed a stormy day. Having escaped the perils of that day, we had sought out a quiet, secret camping location, to hide from the eyes of men like thieves, not even daring to light a fire. Now, four weeks later, we were again camping, for the last time, under a starlit sky, also at the full moon. But how the conditions had changed.

After sunset we reached a small copse by the side of the road, in a pretty little location where a fire burned brightly, and where I could see various cooking vessels. A lot of people seemed to be in a good mood there, and I said: 'I must see who those people are, they seem to be having a good time.' I got down from the wagon and walked over to them. I was astonished to find my previous Israelite travelling companions. They were also surprised and greeted me with joy when they saw who I was.

'Well, this is going to be a fine evening and we can all swap our memories!'

One of them drew a fine coffee set from his wagon and coffee was prepared, as they knew that I liked it. We added to the meal from our supplies and later we made grog. We were all very relaxed and the evening turned into a party, which went on until late in the night.

It is always a pleasant experience, in such a hazardous situation, to meet people who exhibit such loyalty. That is what these merchants did whenever I met them, and it was never with any selfish motivation.

It may have pleased them that I had showed none of the prejudice that is generally shown in society to the Jews. This was not hard for me; I have always seen only the human being in a man, without regard for religion, nationality or class, and have always found it easy to make friends as soon as I recognised a good heart and fine feelings in anyone. This policy has never let me down.

The day after this meeting with the Jews (who begged me to stay with them if I should ever get to Glogau) I finally reached the sizeable town of Minsk. It was the evening of 23 October.

I stayed here for some days, to put some matters in order; to sell my horses (for a real song), because there was no way that I would be able to get on with those poor animals. I could not expect to get new horses, so there was nothing for it but to go on to Vilna by post-horse. The day after my arrival I called on the governor, who received me in friendly fashion and talked with me for a long time. He gave my papers to an officer of his staff, in order to have them signed and to make out the necessary passes so that I could get post-horses. When I had returned to my lodgings, I noticed that he had given me a route card which took me via Vilna and Königsberg, and listed every post station through which I had to pass. The marching order was the same. I went straight back to the governor and pointed out this error; I had asked to be allowed to return through Grodno and Warsaw.

He looked at me seriously and said, very clearly: 'There is no mistake; this is what I intended. You cannot take that route! Go the way that I have given you. I wish you a pleasant journey!'

I could see from his manner, that there was nothing to be done. 'Odd behaviour by this man. Why on earth does he want me to make such a diversion?' I said to myself. Then I bowed to the inevitable and set off. It soon became clear why I had been given this route in Minsk. Some days after I left the place, the advanced guard of the Russian army under Chichagov's command, out of Turkey, appeared close to the town. And on the second night of my journey to Vilna, the post commander was unwilling to give me any horses, as there were rumours that there were cossacks in the area. If I had taken the road to Grodno, I would have run straight into their arms.

On that second night, before I reached Vilna, I had the most wonderful and joyful adventure of my entire journey. We were still two stations from Vilna, when I came to the post-house to change horses. In front of me was a loaded carriage, which attracted my attention, as the silhouette seemed familiar to me. But I thought no more of it and went into the post-house to register my name in the Post Book, as was required, until my horses had been changed. On the long benches, which ran round the walls, lay two officers covered in blue greatcoats. I thought no more of them and didn't want to disturb them, but I asked who they were. I was told that they were a French general and an officer of cuirassiers, who had arrived an hour beforehand. I climbed into my carriage and soon fell asleep, dreaming of my dear de Saive, when I was woken by a shout from outside my vehicle.

I couldn't believe my ears and thought that I was still dreaming, but again and again I heard: 'Monsieur Adam! Monsieur Adam!'

I threw back the leather curtain of the wagon and saw the valet of my friend de Saive. He told me that his master had woken up just after I left and had signed his name under mine in the Post Book. He had ordered him to saddle up a courier horse at once and to ride after me until he caught me up.

He added that de Saive was beside himself with joy at this wonderful coincidence. He would follow and hoped to catch me at the next post-house. Anyone who understands the deep feelings that existed between me and this nobleman, who understood the emotions that attached me to him, the significant moments of my life that he had shared with me, always there at my side as partner and protector, will have some faint idea of the joy which I felt when I heard this in the middle of the night in a foreign land. Was it the familiar shape of the coach, in which I had so often travelled, was it the two sleeping figures, which attracted my attention, or was it the mental image of de Saive of whom I was just dreaming? I don't know myself, but it was a wonderful meeting, with all the surrounding circumstances. From then on I travelled at a walk, but it was not until we reached the next post-house that we met.

The joy of our unexpected meeting was indescribable. From there we travelled together on to Vilna. Here, I spent the three happiest days of my journey; they went all too quickly. We had such a lot to tell each other! How many memories of happier days were awakened in these rest days. But dark thoughts for the future and for the fate of the army cast a dark shadow over our meeting.

De Saive had been sent by Prince Eugene to Vilna on business and was to stay there when I left after those three days. Vilna is a very fine town, and the quality of life which existed there was of the liveliest; a great confluence of all sorts of troops. You could get anything here if you had the money. I improved parts of my costume and bought a new hat; I could not be seen anywhere in my old one.

To continue the journey with post-horses seemed to me to be too expensive. I feared that my supply of cash would run out. I thus made a contract with a Jew, to drive us to Königsberg for 40 thalers. These people do all sorts of business, especially transportation. He had five horses, harnessed abreast, and we really moved along. This Jew, I should say, was gifted with endless plots and stories, as are most people of his sort. You could well have believed that he had taken lessons from an Italian intriguer.

Luckily, I had learned how to handle such fellows; on one or two occasions it came to blows, as there was no other way to solve the impasse. Then we made it up again. It was always about money and swindling.

I had left my Polish servant in Vilna; he soon found a new master, with whom he went to Paris. Three years later, he visited me in Munich.

We left Vilna on 28 October, reached the Niemen at Kovno, and carried on up the right bank of the river to Tilsit. Here we left Russia. I shall never forget the wonderful feeling that I had when I bade farewell to the Russian border post. There is little to tell of our journey from Vilna to Tilsit, even though it took us eight days. We usually had bad lodgings and bad roads, but the weather was still very fine. To my great joy, we met up with the baggage of the Crown Prince of Württemberg on the road again.

On 5 November we arrived in Tilsit. With the first step on the left bank of the Niemen, we were back on the soil of our German homeland, which we greeted with a joy and happiness that can only be understood by those who have lived among foreigners for a long time.

After a number of adventures, all of which concluded happily, we reached Munich on 23 December 1812.

Select Bibliography

Adam, Albrecht. *Voyage pittoresque et militaire de Willenberg en Prusse jusqu'a Moscou en 1812*. Munich, 1828.

Bacler d'Albe, Baron Louis-Albert-Guislain. *Souvenirs pittoresques*. 2 vols. Paris, 1898. Bacler was attached to the Topographical Department of Napoleon's headquarters. In addition to wonderful views of Spain he also produced material on the Russian campaign.

Beauharnais, Eugene. *Mémoires et correspondance politique et militaire du Prince Eugène*. Paris, 1858–60, 10 vols. Edited by Baron A. du Casse. This is the authority on the mind and manners of Napoleon's stepson. Eugene is revealed as a man of principle and an able administrator.

Bertolini, Bartolomeo. *La Mia Prigionia*. Trieste, 1859. The memoirs of an Italian officer captured during the retreat.

Buettner, Korporal. *Beschreibung der schirksals des ehmaligen Korporals Buettner währ. sein. 19 monatigen Gefangenschaft in Russland 1812/1813*. Nuremburg, 1831. One of the Bavarian light cavalrymen attached to Eugene's corps; these horsemen feature in Adam's plates.

Caulaincourt, General Armande de. *Mémoires du général de Caulaincourt, duc de Vicenze*. 3 vols. Paris, 1933. Translated as (volume 1) *Memoirs of General de Caulaincourt*, London, 1935; and (volume 2) *No Peace with Napoleon*, London, 1936. One of the best memoirs and certainly the one which reveals the most about Napoleon's thoughts and actions in 1812.

Faber du Faur, G. de. *La Campagne de Russie d'après le journal illustré d'un témoin oculaire*. Paris, 1895. Translated as *With Napoleon in Russia*. London, 2002. A Württemberg artillery officer and professional soldier who was also an artist.

Labaume, Eugene. *Rélation circonstanciée de la campagne de Russie*. Paris, 1814. Translated as *A Circumstantial Narrative of the Campaign in Russia*. London, 1814. Adam's colleague attached to the Topographical Department of IV Corps wrote this work which condemns the expedition in no uncertain terms.

Langeron, Général. *Mémoires de Langeron, général d'infanterie dans l'armée russe. Campagnes de 1812, 1813, 1814*. Paris, 1902. A French officer, who fled the Revolution and ended up in the Russian army. A superb evocation of the disaster which befell Napoleon's army from the Russian point of view.

Laugier, Césare de. *Gl'italiani in Russia per servire alla storia della Russia, della Polonia e dell'Italia nel 1812*. 4 vols. Milan, 1826–7. Laugier was one of the Italian Guards of Honour, a unit which features in Adam's plates and text. He was an enthusiastic soldier but his optimism was quickly tempered by the ordeal of the retreat.

Lejeune, Baron Louis Francois. *Mémoires du général Lejeune*. Paris, Firmin-Didot, 1896, 2 vols. Translated as *The Memoirs of Baron Lejeune*, London, 1897. A superb account by an experienced soldier.

Muraldt, Albrecht von. *Beresina*. Bern, 1942. An account by a Bavarian cavalryman. He focuses on the retreat.

Rodozhitskii, Ilya Timofeyovitch. *Pokhodnye zapiski artillerista, s 1812 po 1816 god*. Moscow, 1835. An honest and detailed account by a Russian artillery officer. Every bit as good as the memoirs of his French contemporaries.

Schubert, F. von. *Unter dem Doppeladler: Erinnerungen eines Deutschen im Russischen Offiziersdienst, 1789–1814*. Stuttgart, 1962. A young German officer attached to the Russian staff.

Soltyk, Comte Roman. *Napoléon en 1812. Mémoires historiques et militaires sur la campagne de Russie*. Paris, 1836. A Polish Topographical officer with a sharp, observant eye and deep-seated enthusiasm for war on Russia.

Tascher, Maurice de. *Notes de campagne (1806–1813)*. Chateauroux, 1938. Tascher kept a journal and his experiences portray the emotions of a reluctant soldier. It is a highly moving and disturbing account of one man's war.

Tchicherin, Aleksander Vasilevich. *Dnevnik Aleksandra Tchicherina, 1812–1813*. Moscow, 1966. A Russian soldier who kept a sketchbook of scenes of Russian army life.

Vaudoncourt, Frédéric Guillaume de. *Critical Situation of Bonaparte in his retreat out of Russia, by an Eye-witness*. London, 1815. Vaudoncourt was with IV Corps and his dry account was one of the very first to be published.